TRANSFORMED BY *Love*

Testimonies to Bring Hope
to Struggling Hearts

Lem, Linda
& Mom
Praying you will
be blessed as you
read these stories
Love you All
Viola

Viola Grant

Printed in Canada

ISBN: 978-1-4866-0914-7

Word Alive Press
131 Cordite Road, Winnipeg, MB R3W 1S1
www.wordalivepress.ca

MIX
Paper from
responsible sources
FSC® C103567

Library and Archives Canada Cataloguing in Publication

Grant, Viola, 1946-, author
        Transformed by love : testimonials to bring hope to
struggling hearts / Viola Grant.

Issued in print and electronic formats.
ISBN 978-1-4866-0914-7 (paperback).--ISBN 978-1-4866-0915-4 (pdf).--
ISBN 978-1-4866-0916-1 (html).--ISBN 978-1-4866-0917-8 (epub)

        1. Addicts--Religious life. 2. Substance abuse--Religious aspects--
Christianity. 3. Christian life. I. Title.

BV4596.A24G73 2016   248.8'629   C2016-900050-8

                                                   C2016-900051-6

contents

dedication

I want to dedicate this book to my parents. My father, Stanley Gates, passed away several years ago, but he was always supportive of anything I did for God, and I know he would be very happy about this book. My mother, Frances Gates, has been the best mother anyone could have, and also my very best friend. She always understood me and encouraged me, and she loved to talk about God and His Word. Today she lives in a nursing home and is suffering with bone cancer and Alzheimer's. I can no longer communicate with her, but her love, concern, and compassion will live on forever in my heart.

acknowledgements

First of all, I want to give thanks to God, for if I didn't have Him to depend on, this book would not have been written. Through all the disappointments and problems, and the many times when I wanted to quit, He always brought someone along who would confirm that I was doing exactly what He wanted. I love you, Lord!

To my husband, Ronald—Thank you for loving and supporting me through this journey. Thank you for always being by my side as we made the trips to the homes of the people we interviewed for this book. Thank you for reminding me so many times that it was not my book, but God's, because He was the one who asked me to do it. You have truly been an inspiration and a blessing! I love you!

To my son, Tony—You have helped me greatly with all of your technical knowledge and skills. Thank you for believing in me. You have truly been a blessing. Love you!

Thank you to Pastor Paul McPhail for taking time out of your very busy schedule to do the author bio for this book. Thank you for your sermons, which have been such a source of encouragement as I've been on this journey.

Thank you to Pastor Dorman Pollett for writing the Foreword. If I hadn't attended your church, I wouldn't have met a lot of these wonderful people or had the chance to hear their testimonies. Thank God that He always has us where He wants us for His purposes.

Thank you to Pastor Gertrude Armaly of Antioch Christian Ministry for granting me permission to use the name of her conference as the name for this book.

I want to thank all of you who gave me your testimonies. Without you, this book could not have been written. I believe that as people read your testimonies, hope will spring up as they realize that what God has done for you, He can also do for them. As a result, many lives will be transformed.

Thank you to the people at Word Alive Press for your patience and encouragement throughout this writing process.

foreword

I want to congratulate Viola Grant, the author of this book. Her determination to tell what God has done in the lives of others began when she was about fourteen years old. Living in Newfoundland, there were fishermen and their families who would leave their homes for the summer months and go to other places where there were better fishing grounds. Viola's family went every summer for many years to a small community called Fishot Islands, which was made up of many small islands. Viola realized there was no Sunday school for all those children who were there for the summer, and she felt God would have her start one. The first problem, because there were no cars, was to find a way to get the children to and from her Sunday school. She believed asking her dad for the use of his rowboat would be a challenge, but he lovingly gave her his permission.

Every Sunday for the remainder of the summer, she would row to three of the small islands to pick up the children from one island at a time and take them to her family cottage. She would do Sunday school with the help of some of the older children, and then take them all back to their homes again. Sometimes the wind would be so high that by the time Viola had picked up and delivered the children to their homes, every finger on both hands would be sore with blisters from trying to row against the wind.

That determination was sparked again a few years ago, when Viola and her husband started attending our church in Wheatley, Ontario. At that time, we were busing men and women from Windsor, Ontario to our church. It didn't take long for Viola to get involved, especially in the Saturday Family Day program at the Salvation Army Rehabilitation Centre in Windsor. Some of the men and women who are sharing their testimonies in this book are people Viola came to know personally. Her hard work, many phone calls, and visits to conduct interviews to get the needed information for this book is to be commended. These stories need to be heard and read.

I would liken Viola to a woman in the Bible who said, "*If I may but touch His garment, I shall be whole,*" (Matthew 9:21). I believe Viola's intent to be the same as that woman's. Seeing the wholeness that has come to so many men and women through the touch of the Master, and being able to share their stories in her book, is her way of touching Jesus. She shows people what God can do when we reach out to Him.

Thank you, Viola, for your passion, faithfulness, and obedience. May God richly bless you with many changed lives as they read the life-changing testimonies in this book.

Pastor Dorman Pollett Sr.

For years whenever I saw someone who was addicted to drugs or alcohol, I would wonder why they had to be like that—that is, until a few years ago, when my husband and I attended Wheatley Evangel church in Wheatley, Ontario. The senior pastor, Pastor Dorman Pollett, told us about a family day-program at the Salvation Army Rehabilitation Centre in Windsor, Ontario, for recovering addicts. My husband and I were interested in attending. We eventually fell in love with the people there, and for many months we attended this program every second Saturday. Through the teachings and presentations, we learned a lot about the disease of alcoholism and other addictions. More than our learning, which was very important, we looked forward to being able to support and bless the people in that room. We also looked forward to being with them and hearing their stories. In many cases, their families had given up on them, and even though this day was called Family Day, most of them would have no family there. We began to feel very much like family. It was truly awesome!

Around that time, I'd been considering writing my life's story, but the Holy Spirit interrupted my plans by telling me to put my story on hold and to write the testimonies of the people I'd met, and would meet, at the program. The pages of this book are the true stories of people who've had many terrible things happen to them but have been changed by God, and today they are pastors, entrepreneurs, and other contributing members of society.

I pray that as you read these pages and see what God has done for these people, you will be filled with hope for yourself and your loved ones, especially anyone who seems hopeless. The

God who helped and blessed the people in these pages is still the God of today, and He can help and heal any wounded heart.

Lord, I pray in Jesus' name, touch and heal each person who is reading this book, whether their need is for physical, mental, emotional, or spiritual help. Nothing is impossible with you, Lord. Praise your name!

At the Lowest

Point of His Life,

God Got His

Attention

Dorman was born on March 12, 1976, to Dorman and Cindy Pollett. He is the oldest of four children: two brothers and one sister. Dorman was raised in a Christian home in a small town in Newfoundland called New Harbour. His father was a fisherman, and his mother worked in a fish plant.

Dorman accepted Christ into his life when he was seven or eight years old. Even as a child, he cared about others. On a career day in Kindergarten, he dressed in a three-piece suit and carried a sign saying "Preacher," which was really a "sign of prophecy," but we will hear more about that later. His role model was Steve Pardy, a well-known gospel singer in Newfoundland, which is not surprising considering that Dorman's whole family is very musically inclined. In 1988, on his twelfth birthday, Dorman moved with his family to Ontario.

When Dorman was thirteen years old, his uncle died. This uncle had always been his hero, so it was quite a traumatic event for him. At this time, he took his first drink of alcohol. When he was fifteen years old, he attended a youth conference called "Carry the Torch." Here he received a word of knowledge that said, "Your uncle died, and you fell away from Christ," which was exactly what happened.

At sixteen years of age, Dorman started working at Circle Square Ranch in Severn Bridge, Ontario. He loved working with the children, especially teaching them to ride horses. During the same year that he started to drink socially, he quit high school and began working in the construction industry. When he was nineteen years old, he started driving trucks and began to take "border beans," which were pills to help him stay awake. This progressed to crystal meth and crack cocaine. There were times when he didn't sleep for five or six days, or even as long as nine days. At this point he would start hallucinating. He became so hooked on these drugs that he started selling them to help support his habit.

At the age of twenty, he married and had two beautiful children: a boy named DJ, and a girl, Julie. Because of his drug habit, he and his wife split up a couple of times. Eventually, while living in Ontario, his wife called him at a crack house and gave him an ultimatum—drugs or family. Dorman hung up the phone and continued to use, which resulted in the failure of his marriage. Soon he realized that he'd lost his family, his home, and his business. Everything was gone. He'd hit rock bottom! He got on his motorcycle and drove to his parents' house. His dad was waiting for him in the driveway, and his mom was at the door. Dorman finally admitted his situation to them: "Mom and Dad, I can't do it anymore ... I need help."

They took Dorman to see Pastor Jeff Johns, Prophet Johnnie Beard, and Prophet Phil Rich, who at that time were ministering at Antioch Ministries. Pastor Johnnie, with no idea what was happening with Dorman, put his hand on Dorman's chest and prophesied: Surely DJ (Dorman's son) would grow up and say, "Surely my dad is a man of God."

Dorman then went to a friend's home in Indiana where he detoxed. From there, he went to Teen Challenge in Midland, Texas, for one week before heading back to his friend's home in Indiana. One night after his family had returned to Newfoundland, and at the very lowest point of his life, he couldn't sleep. Around 3:00 a.m. he finally said, "Ok, God, you have my attention. What do you want?"

God replied: "I don't want your attention. I want you, Dorman."

"I give it all up, Lord, but I need to feel you like I've never felt you before." Suddenly, he felt somebody sit on his bed; he felt arms go underneath and around him, and he heard the words, "Son, I've got you."

"In my darkest hour," Dorman explains today, "when I had nothing to live for, Jesus came and met me right where I was— and I have never been the same."

Dorman came back to Ontario and did the forty-day residential addiction program at the Salvation Army Rehabilitation Centre in Windsor, Ontario. Around a year later, Dorman's children came to visit from Newfoundland. Dorman told his son, DJ, of his vision to open a rehabilitation centre.

"I can help with that," DJ said. When Dorman asked him how he could help, DJ replied, "When we lost everything and had to move back to Newfoundland, I was really mad at you, so I can help little boys who are mad at their dads. I can help them to love them again."

While Dorman was at the rehabilitation centre in Windsor, he met Erica Ennis, one of the volunteers. Erica was a single mom of four beautiful children: Chelsea, Hannah, Levi, and Mia.

"Erica came as a guest speaker, and I fell in love with her the first time I saw her," Dorman explains. They felt that

God was calling both of them to the same ministry—to work with addicts. A year and a half later, they became engaged; six months after that, they were married. Erica's four children and Dorman's two children blended together very quickly. God has blessed Dorman and Erica immensely. They are best friends and inseparable.

July of 2010 saw the realization of the truth of the sign Dorman carried on his Kindergarten career day, which proclaimed him as a "Preacher." In that month, he was licensed with the Independent Assemblies of God International and later ordained. In 2011, he was also ordained with Whitehorse Christian Center in Indiana.

At an Independent Assemblies of God conference in November, 2010, Dr. Russ Moyer prophesied that Dorman would have a prophetic ministry of evangelism and healing gifts with signs and wonders. God started using him in a prophetic ministry in mid-summer of 2011.

Dorman and his wife, Erica, have founded a ministry called "Carry the Torch Ministry," which is exactly what they have already started doing as they reach out to others using the many gifts and abilities that God has given them. They attend Wheatley Evangel Tabernacle in Wheatley, Ontario, where Dorman's dad, Pastor Dorman Pollett Sr., is the senior pastor. Dorman often ministers in song. He also plays the drums, and he and Erica are always available to do the preaching whenever needed. Many doors are beginning to open for them to minister in churches in other communities.

God has performed many miracles in Dorman's life, bringing him from his days as a drug addict to his role as a preacher of the gospel of Christ with dreams to open an addiction rehabilitation centre as well as a home for single mothers and their children. He would like to say to anyone who is now where he was in addiction: "It's a one-way road to nowhere. The only thing waiting for you is jail or death. The only way I found freedom was through Jesus, and "*if the Son therefore shall make you free, ye shall be free indeed*," (John 8:36).

I Wanted to Die,

Because

I Didn't Know

How to Live

Leah[1]* was born in Windsor, Ontario, where she attended a Catholic church and school. She grew up with two brothers and two sisters and her mom and dad. Her parents did the best they could, but because of work commitments, they had very little time for their children. The kids were never told they were loved or appreciated. Because of the physical, emotional, and sexual abuse meted out by her dad, Leah developed violent tendencies. She was around seven years old when the abuse started. Her dad was an alcoholic and was usually drunk when it happened.

School proved to be a place where Leah also suffered much physical and emotional abuse. Her teachers made her feel like she was stupid and would never amount to anything. She received this message at home as well. She felt so misunderstood.

As she grew into her teenage years, Leah became very shy and withdrawn. When she was thirteen years old, she and a group of her girlfriends started attending church in the morning. She realizes now that even back then there was a spiritual hunger within her.

---

[1]* Not her real name

Soon after she turned fourteen, her family moved to the Toronto area. She says that it was at this point the sexual abuse stopped, but the physical abuse increased. Leah became very jealous of her two sisters, because they were her father's favourites. She says she felt defective, because the only attention she received was abusive, and she began to use food as a way to deal with this.

At sixteen, Leah began having migraine headaches, which would often cause hospitalization. This was one way she would get attention, and she learned to manipulate the system. School was very difficult at this time, and during grades seven and eight, she grew to hate her teachers and the whole school system. She finished school, but felt as if she'd been pushed through. She feared doing exams, but with determination and the help of God, she made it.

By the time Leah turned eighteen, she began having more health issues, and because of all the abuse, she also suffered from depression. She became very resentful and unforgiving, all of which eventually led her down the path of alcohol and drugs, which then made her even more ill. At the same time, all the attention she received from being ill was helping to meet her emotional needs. She says that during this time she was trying to fill the empty void inside of her, and by age twenty-nine, she was a full-fledged alcohol/drug addict.

The next few years saw Leah in and out of addiction treatment centres eight times. During her last time, she was told to "get out" because she wasn't doing what it would take for her to get the help she needed. That was her wake-up call. She knew that if she wanted to live, she desperately needed to change her lifestyle. She was sent to a women's program where she was finally able to turn her life around. She also started attending two "Twelve Step" programs: one to help with the alcohol addiction, and one to help with the drug addiction. While coming off drugs and alcohol, and because of her addictive behaviour, Leah began to smoke cigarettes. At the same time, she was in and out of hospital and began seeing a psychiatrist, because she had become very suicidal and had started to self-abuse.

"I simply felt like I wanted to die," she says, "because I didn't know how to live. Once I was stabilized with medications, I eventually developed a desire to live and find my purpose."

After two years of meetings and professional help, Leah had finally overcome the addiction of alcohol and drugs and was at last sober.

Even though she was no longer doing drugs or alcohol, she still felt there was something missing in her life. She felt very lonely and desperate, but because of her trust issues, she couldn't confide in anyone. She desperately needed someone she could talk to who would understand her. She needed help breaking down walls she had built around herself to keep from being hurt again. Because of her Catholic upbringing, she knew about God. She began watching other people who seemed happy, and she realized there was something different in their lives. She began asking questions, which eventually led her to call on God for help. She recognized as well that someone bigger than her was helping her stay sober.

A friend recommended to Leah that she start attending a Bible-based church, but because of her weight, asthma, need for a wheelchair, and other health issues, she felt unable to attend. Around this time, though, a pastor's wife began visiting her and talking to her about Jesus. Eventually she was able to attend church, and on her very first Sunday, she felt Jesus say to her, "You are home."

Still not totally grounded in the faith or in the teaching of God's Word, she found herself once again having suicidal thoughts and abusing herself. With much love from her church family, and more importantly with the help of God, she slowly learned to live again. She eventually received complete healing and no longer needed the wheelchair; she gives glory to God for this. She lost a lot of her weight when she had gastric bypass surgery. This was a real time of testing for her, but God saw her through and the surgery was a success.

In an effort to grow in grace and learn more about God, she now attends two women's Bible studies. She recently graduated from a Christian rehabilitation program called "Stepping Stones," where she received a lot of help and encouragement. She has now "Stepped Up" as a mentor to other women in the program.

Much to Leah's amazement, her dad dropped by for a coffee one day, and God gave her the strength to confront him about the abuse of the past. Everything finally came out in the open. Her dad apologized, and now she is able to say that she has a love for her dad like never before. By the grace of God, she has been able to totally forgive him.

Today Leah has hopes and dreams that she once thought were impossible.

"I no longer believe I am a nobody," she explains. "I know I am a king's kid. All things are new, and I believe I can do all things through Christ."

For those who are going through circumstances similar to Leah's, she would like to remind them of the words of Jesus in Matthew 22:37: "*Thou shalt love the Lord thy God with all thy heart, and with all thy soul, and with all thy mind.*" She wants people to know that God has been with her, even in the darkest hours of her life, and He will help them, too, if they will seek Him.

He Was

Repeatedly Told

He Was

a Nobody

David was born in Point Pelee, Ontario. As a child, he found living there very exciting, because there was always something to do. He says his parents were good people. His mother believed boys should be gentlemen and required stronger discipline than girls. His dad drank, but when drunk he would become funny rather than mean or violent. David didn't have a good relationship with his siblings. He says he was the youngest and always seemed to get the short end of the stick. He felt a lot of pressure from the older siblings and was repeatedly told by them that he was a nobody. As a result, he was constantly made to feel that everybody else was more important than him.

At ten years of age, David smoked his first cigarette; at fifteen, he began using drugs in what he describes as "a small way." His brother wanted him to try some drugs so that David couldn't "tattle" on him. There was always a fear of retaliation. His siblings' attitude was, "Unless you are equally guilty, you may 'tattle' on us, so we'll make you do whatever we're doing."

His siblings had nothing else to do except tease, and their teasing was often aimed at David. This continued in school when he chose not to take part in sports but to play other games instead. This led the other students to view David and his friends as weird. At school, he was under constant pressure to conform to what other people thought was normal. The most pressure came from people who believed he was doing wrong activities and spending time with the wrong friends. He and his friends were considered "geeks." David reached a point where he felt he would either "explode" or "implode" (recede within himself and have nothing else to do with anyone). Around this time, he even considered doing harm to his school, and he had many suicidal thoughts. Because of the hurt he experienced in his earlier years, he made very little effort to date or get to know girls. He didn't want to be vulnerable and give anyone else power to hurt him anymore.

He was around eighteen years of age when he landed his first job. At this point he really started to use drugs, because now he had the money to buy them. He says he began using drugs because he'd always felt so bad and known so much hurt, and the drugs made him feel good and happy. He discovered, however, that the drugs made him feel good for only about an hour the first time, and then every other time they became less and less effective and required a higher amount until they deadened the emotions. Even those deadened emotions felt better than all the hurt and fear he'd been accustomed to. Eventually, he measured everything in terms of "getting high."

David's drug use escalated to the point where most of his cheques were going to buy drugs instead of food and clothing and other essentials. He did, however, continue to pay his rent and other bills. David started renting with another guy, but within two months he'd moved out to go and live with his girlfriend, leaving David with the entire rent. About six months later, David's brother moved in. He ate any extra food and felt that he was "lord of the manor," but David was responsible for all the bills. All of David's hurt feelings from the past were renewed at an even higher level, and things went from bad to worse. By the time they'd lived together for five years, David's brother was not only stealing David's food, but his money also. Because of this, David didn't have enough money left for rent, so he decided to move in with a friend, who was also a drug user. There was a lot of drugs and partying, but he felt that it was an improvement over his past situation.

A couple of years later, David moved in with another brother, who guaranteed there would be no abuse and that they would split the cost of the bills. This brother eventually got a girlfriend who moved in with them. She became "number one," and David again felt like a nobody.

Over the next twenty years, things just seemed to spiral out of control for him. Both he and his brother were doing drugs and were on the verge of poverty. His brother's girlfriend was pressuring them to spend less on drugs, but they decided that the best solution was to start selling drugs, but only to friends. This seemed to work for a while. They were eating well, but also able to stay as "high" as they wanted.

Everything seemed to be going great until one of their friends turned out to be working for the RCMP. David awoke one morning to a police officer pointing a gun at his head and telling him to "freeze." He and his brother spent the morning in jail. When they got home, they decided there was no place in their house for drugs. Supporting each other, and with much inspiration from his brother's girlfriend, they were both able to quit the drugs altogether. His brother was charged by the RCMP, because he was the one in charge of the household and holding the money. David was charged, but he didn't have to go to trial. His brother was told that he would have to attend

Narcotics Anonymous. Because of the help he received there, he got better, while David continued to "pity party." His brother kept inviting him to Narcotics Anonymous, and after a year David finally attended an open meeting, just so his brother would stop nagging him.

The speaker at David's first Narcotics Anonymous meeting was half his age and full of tattoos and body piercings, so David assumed he had nothing to say that would be of interest or help. When the speaker finally did share, it was as if he was telling David's story. There were so many similarities that David wondered if his brother had told the speaker his story. David was so confused, he decided to attend one more meeting to figure it all out.

David says that at this point in his life he had a terrible attitude. He was certain he was much more intelligent than anyone else there and that nobody could teach him anything. The next meeting was a closed one, where everyone was invited to share their story. He sat at a "first-step" table, which meant he would be in a discussion of how drugs made life unmanageable.

"That night six people told my story before I had a chance to share it," David says.

Because of his upbringing, David was in the habit of keeping his thoughts to himself, for fear of letting others know his weaknesses.

"At first, I tried to fake it through my story, but out of sheer panic, I honestly shared some of my inner feelings. Because things didn't happen as usual, meaning that things didn't blow up in my face, and I didn't hear about it on the street the next day, I was encouraged to go back to a third meeting. At this point, I began to attend regularly, but still held on to bad attitudes."

Some months into recovery, David noticed that people who had gone to fewer meetings than he had were actually having more success than him. He questioned the leaders about this and was told that people who do what they are told from the beginning get much better results than those who don't. He decided he'd better start taking responsibility for his own situation instead of blaming everyone else, which led him to make the changes in his life that would get him to a new level.

"As I started taking instruction, I noticed that I began to live again instead of just trying to exist, and I was better able to accept that other people desired to help me without wanting anything in return. I began to have faith in others and myself."

David first attended church at the age of seven. He was confirmed and also became an altar boy; however, he still felt all the pressures of life, so he assumed God wasn't willing to help him. When drugs came along, he finally felt happy. This happiness diminished somewhat when he realized that going to church and doing drugs at the same time made him feel uncomfortable, so he decided he couldn't do both. He chose to give up church instead of the drugs.

When David started attending Narcotics Anonymous and began to feel better about himself, he desired to have God in his life again. He says he probably shared this desire in the meetings but didn't act on it until someone finally faced him and said, "Next Sunday morning I'll pick you up for church." He didn't want to embarrass himself, and he really did desire to go, so he agreed. That Sunday he found himself at the Salvation Army for the first time in his life. He wasn't exactly comfortable with all the singing, but he decided to continue attending. Very early on, the pastor talked about the day when all of God's people from all denominations would gather together in heaven, and this really impressed David. He was also very impressed with all the good works the Salvation Army did in the community for all people, not just their own.

"After a while I began to feel I was part of a real family who loved and cared about each other. They showed me so much love and concern. This really helped me break down the barriers of fear and distrust in people."

After two years at his new church and five years at Narcotics Anonymous, David was able to break free from the nicotine addiction and quit smoking cigarettes. He says being involved with both the church and Narcotics Anonymous helped bring more purpose and direction to his life. He believes God has a strange sense of humour, because although he wanted to go back to church, he wanted to go to the one he'd attended previously. However, now he believes that God led him to the Salvation Army and has purposely worked all things for his (David's) good and God's glory, as the Bible says in Romans 8:28: "*And we know that all things work together for good to them that love God, to them who are the called according to His purpose.*"

David has been drug free for about twenty-five years, and he has no desire to ever be involved with drugs again.

"Life is still a struggle at times, but I now have someone who helps me every step of the way." One of his favourite sayings is, "If God brings you to it, He will bring you through it." David now lives life to the fullest. "There is no struggle so great that God and a sense of humour can't handle," he proclaims.

To anyone reading this who is going through any kind of a struggle, David wants to say: "What you have been through or are presently going through can make you stronger, if you give God the opportunity to work all things out for you. God is faithful."

He Had No Idea

Why He Was Doing This,

but Now Knows God

Had a Plan

George[2*] was born on November 3, 1960, in Ontario. He was the second youngest of seven kids. He lived with his family on a two-and-a-half-acre hobby farm with many animals, which made his early years interesting.

When George was only eight years old, he smoked his first marijuana joint, which was given to him by his brothers. At age nine, he was allowed his first beer. He could always have one beer on special occasions. He was raised in a good family with great parents.

In public school, he was introduced to drugs and alcohol. He and his school buddies would actually start their "drugs and drinking" day while on their way to school on the bus. By the time they got to school, they were already drunk. In high school, George was doing many different kinds of drugs and also alcohol. He says he doesn't have memories of many things during those years because of all the drinking and drugs.

In 1979, his mom and dad moved to another community in Ontario, and he went with them to help with the move. His

---

[2*] Not his real name.

dad wanted him to stay to do some hunting and fishing. At that time, he started dating the woman he would spend the next thirty years with. They had three boys together, but only one of them has kept in touch with him. Throughout his marriage and while raising three children, George continued to drink and do drugs, including cocaine.

One day in 2010, he had an argument with his wife. About an hour later, while at work, he received a text message from her saying that his son was in the hospital. A little later, he got another message saying his son was home, so he stayed at work. After work, he went to a bar with his buddies and became very intoxicated. He walked home and passed out on the couch. His wife came home and another argument took place, but this time she called the police. George soon woke up to two police officers. They handcuffed him and took him off to jail, where he remained for twenty days. At George's trial, the judge told him that if he stayed in jail for another ten days he could go free, but he'd have to participate in several courses, two of which were Anger Management and Narcotics Anonymous.

The morning after his release, George went to pick up his cheque at work, where a temptation awaited him.

"You're still on the clock," his supervisor said. "Go and get us a round of beer."

George got the victory over that temptation when he told the supervisor he wouldn't get the beer because he was on probation and needed to stay away from all drugs and alcohol.

George then went to his case worker and told her that he wanted to go to Windsor. She quite willingly transferred all his files to a case worker in Windsor. George recounts that when he got on the bus that would bring him to Windsor, he had no idea why he was doing it, but now he knows that God had a plan. He started going to Alcoholics Anonymous meetings, where he heard about Narcotic Anonymous meetings being held at the Salvation Army Rehabilitation Centre. He went to the centre to check things out and was told about the addictions program there.

In less than three months, George had attended one hundred and sixty meetings and was able to complete enough papers for his probation. Even though he had seven months of probation left, his probation officer was so impressed with him that he told George he didn't need to check in with him again, except to sign a couple of papers.

In 2011, George started attending Lazarus House's "Family Stepping Stones" program. He says that because of all the help and encouragement given to him by the facilitator of that program, he accepted the Lord into his life and got baptized.

"At the time of my baptism," he relates, "there was a real sense of the presence of the Holy Spirit. Growing up, there was no encouragement towards attending church, so I never understood anything about God and His love. Life now has new meaning and purpose."

His message for others who find themselves doing drugs and alcohol is this: "Change your life by giving your heart to the Lord, and He will help you to overcome, just as He did for me. Today I live a much happier, contented life, and it's all because of what God has done for me. I am so thankful to God, to my program facilitator, and to the many others whom God has brought into my life to influence, encourage, and bless me."

Being at Rock Bottom

Didn't Stop Him

from Becoming a

Successful Entrepreneur

James was born on November 6, 1982. He is an only child. He lived with both parents prior to his dad's death when James was only seven years old. His dad had been an alcoholic, and his mom drank as well, but he says he only saw her drink on weekends. She was a good mom and did what she could for him. When he was around twelve, he started hanging out with the wrong crowd and really gave his mom a hard time. When he was fifteen and in high school, his friends all smoked marijuana and drank, so he started to do the same.

The next year, his mom got sick. The doctors discovered that she had a malignant brain tumour. She continued to get worse and eventually went into the hospital. James stayed home alone. He would go to school, come home, and then go visit his mom. No one else in the family knew about her sickness, because she didn't want anyone to know. The only person he was able to talk to was an aunt, but he couldn't even tell her about his mom. His mom stayed in the hospital for a month, but a week after she came home, she had a seizure while he was at school, and she couldn't get to a phone. When he got home he called for an ambulance immediately and got her back to the hospital. He then called his uncle, to whom he had not spoken in many years. His uncle and his daughter, James' cousin, came to the hospital. They found it hard to believe that James had been staying alone for so long. James then went to live with his cousin, to whom his mom had given her power of attorney. His mom was soon transferred to the hospital in Ingersoll, which was much closer to him. She continued to get worse and passed away about three months later. He found her passing very difficult, and it was hard to go back to the house that his mom and he had shared to clean out and dispose of her things.

James didn't really know his family, but now he found himself having to live with them, which he also found very difficult. He graduated from high school, however, and went to college to do an apprenticeship in auto body. After one year, he was offered a full-time job with the sponsoring body shop.

He lived with his family for a year. They helped him get his license, but otherwise things didn't go very well. He was drinking and partying and staying out all night—sometimes even for several days. His cousin didn't like this. She'd been in an accident several years earlier and was taking oxycontin and Percocet because of her pain caused by the accident. James started stealing her pills and taking them. He began to build up a tolerance to them, so he needed more and more to get high. Eventually she caught him and kicked him out of her house, but in a week or so he was back again. Everything started to go downhill from there. He lost his license, so he was driving without a license and without insurance. He got tickets that he didn't pay, and he started stealing things from his cousin's house. While working at a body shop at the time, he would steal cars and take the parts off them to sell. He was in and out of jail a lot.

James eventually moved out of his cousin's house and started renting a house from his boss in London. He'd had an accident while driving impaired and totalled his truck, so now had no means of transportation to and from work in London.

While in London, he started working at another body shop. His boss opened a bar next door to the shop, and James started working at the bar. He would borrow money from his boss to pay for his drugs, so by the end of the week when the money was taken out for his rent and to repay his boss for the drug money, there would be no money left, so James was always broke. He met a girl at the bar, and not long after she moved in with him. About two years later, she had a little boy. Shortly after that, James stopped paying his rent and showing up for work, so he lost both his job and his house. Eventually he started working at yet another body shop. The relationship with the girl he met at the bar lasted for about five years before they broke it off.

James had a good friend with whom he used to get into trouble and whose dad allowed him to rent a room in his home. James' only reason for working was to buy drugs. That was all that mattered to him at that time. He was getting into more and more drugs, and needed more and more money, so he started stealing money from his friend's dad. Once he was discovered, he wasn't wanted there anymore, so once again he had no job and no money. He then went to stay at another friend's place, which was only a shell of a house with no insulation. James slept on the plywood floor with only an old coat as a covering. All of his other things were left at the other man's house, and he was afraid to go back and get them for fear of getting into a fight.

The next morning, James started walking ... but he really had no place to go. He went to downtown London to some health place, where he was told to go to the Salvation Army Detox Centre. While walking to the centre, he stopped at a pay phone and called his cousin, but she wanted nothing to do with him. At this point, he hadn't had drugs for a couple of days, and he was beginning to get sick. He had no one and no place to turn to. He says, "I had finally hit rock bottom."

He made it to the detox centre where he was admitted and given a room and bed for eight days. After using drugs such as oxycontin and Percocet for six years, he found this time at the detox centre very difficult. Then something happened that he considers miraculous. He was able to get into the Salvation Army Rehabilitation Centre in Windsor.

James graduated from the rehabilitation program and went into the transition program. While going through the rehabilitation program, he was confined to the centre, but in the transition program, he was able to come and go as he wished.

He eventually moved into an apartment with a friend and started working at odd jobs. Soon he met Dorman Pollett Jr. and started attending Dorman's father's church in Wheatley. Life for James became very interesting. At the church, he met his future wife, Crystal. He also met the Lord and was baptized.

"My life was forever changed," he explains, "and everything started falling into place. Seven months later, I married my beautiful bride, Crystal."

About two years before getting married, he started working at an auto factory installing parts, but he wasn't very happy. He really wanted to work at what he loved—auto body work. Eventually he and a friend who also worked at the same auto factory became risk takers and decided to get their own auto body shop. They rented a place, and because of James' well-known work etiquette, the word soon got around town. He and his friend would work at the auto factory from 6:30 a.m. until

2:30 p.m., and then work at the auto body shop until 2:00 or 3:00 the next morning. They worked like this for about four months, but then decided to quit the car factory and go full time with their auto body shop. Business really started picking up, and James was finally happy doing what he loved.

About one year and two months after their marriage, Crystal and James became parents to a beautiful little girl they named Sophia. Twenty-three months later, they became a family of four when their handsome little boy, Jimmy, arrived.

"Our children are such a blessing to us," James says.

James continues to work hard at "Elite Auto Body," the company that he and his friend started in Windsor, Ontario. He eventually got his driver's license back, finished his apprenticeship, and got his auto body license.

James has been clean (not taken any drugs or alcohol) for eight years. He gives God all the glory and credit for all that has happened in his life. God is good!!

To anyone who is addicted to drugs and/or alcohol, James would say to you: "Give your life to God, and let Him direct your steps. What He's done for me, He can, and will, do for you."

Author's note: James has become a very successful entrepreneur. The last time I stopped by his shop, he was so busy with so many people and cars around that it was impossible to get a parking spot. Way to go, James! We pray God's blessing on you, your business, and your beautiful family.

With God's Help,

I Stopped Smoking

Immediately

John was born on June 26, 1949. He was the middle of three children. He says he had a great upbringing, and his school years were fairly normal.

Just after he turned seventeen years old, John became sick and was diagnosed with both bipolar disorder and schizophrenia. He spent three months in hospital. Two years later, he started smoking, drinking, and doing drugs.

At age twenty-five, John moved out of his family's home to a rental apartment in Toronto. Soon he moved out West, but only for two months before returning to Toronto. In 2003, he moved to Windsor, where he has been ever since.

In Windsor, John lived at the Salvation Army Rehabilitation Centre for one year. There he became friends with another man who introduced him to Pastor Dorman Pollett Sr., who pastors Wheatley Evangel Church. He started going to this church with his friend, and eventually gave his heart to the Lord. That was about six years ago. He quit smoking immediately, and has not had a cigarette since. He has also been sober for about thirty years.

John is now living in a nursing home. He doesn't get out to church anymore, but he says, "I am still trusting the Lord. I am so thankful to Him for helping me so much."

Author's Note: When I first met John, he'd come with a friend to the church I was attending—Wheatley Evangel Church. I found it very difficult to take my eyes off him, because he looked so sick; I thought he would pass out at any moment. I was very concerned for him. He kept attending the church, and Pastor Dorman and the people of the church began to pray for and "love on" this man. He started to gain some weight and looked so much better than he did that first night. This man is another miracle of God's grace! Thank you, Lord, for your redemption and restoration power in the lives of believers.

He Was on the Verge

of Attempting

to End It All,

When He Heard a Voice...

Chris grew up in a dysfunctional family, but he had a sense of God when he was quite young. Whenever his parents fought, he'd hide under his bed and pray. He'd heard about God in the Catholic church he'd attended a few times, but he didn't know Him. Still, when he hid under his bed and prayed, he would feel the presence of God with him.

His childhood was full of violence. He became very mean, because he felt it was the only way to survive. In grade school, he was badly bullied. He explains that later in his school years, "I grew to become a three-hundred-pound bully as well."

A turning point in his life came at the age of twelve when he had a dream that Jesus pulled him out of rushing water into a canoe. For a couple of years after this experience, Chris returned to church, but when things went wrong there, he returned to his life of crime, drugs, and alcohol. He was in and out of jail. In high school, he was quite popular with many friends, but he continued with his lifestyle of partying, drugs, and alcohol.

While in jail at the age of eighteen, Chris accepted the Lord into his life. For the first time, he knew what it was to have peace and to experience the love and goodness of God. He knew that he'd been forgiven and accepted into God's family. Once he was out of jail, he tried turning his life around by attending a couple of different treatment centres. He also found a great church, but after going there a few times, he soon turned his back on God again, believing that it was all a "farce" and just didn't work. Soon he was back to his old lifestyle.

He continued going to a treatment centre called "Turning Point." During one of the meetings, a lady began talking about God. Chris began to curse and tell her what he believed.

"Go to a man of God and work out your issues," she responded.

These words really got to him, so he called the pastor at the church he'd been attending. He'd intended to be mean to the pastor, but after talking to him and listening to him share the love of God, his life was radically changed. For three years, he served God diligently, and he was eventually offered a youth ministry in Delhi, Ontario, which lasted for about six months until things suddenly went wrong. He was so hurt that he decided that if this is church, he wanted nothing to do with it. For the next ten years, he stayed away from church and got heavily into drugs, which caused medical and mental health problems. He attempted suicide several times.

In 2011, he was once again on the verge of attempting to end it all when he heard the voice of the Lord speaking to him. God reminded him of how He had blessed him in times past, and that He was still God and would help him again. He immediately put on a worship tape and began reading the Bible intensely.

"The Spirit of God came into my room and changed my life dramatically," he shares. "I immediately quit smoking and womanizing and began having encounters with God. People began getting saved and healed in my house. This lasted about two years."

In 2012, Chris went back to high school and finished his education. He then enrolled in Immanuel Bible College. He soon had to discontinue classes because of some health issues, but the following year found him back in Bible college again, and this time he finished with an "A" average. During this time, he was being used in ministry. He was preaching on a weekly basis, and people were getting saved, healed, and set free under his ministry.

There is an obvious call on this man's life, but just as obvious are his struggles. However, he is very optimistic that God's will for his life will prevail, and that his life will demonstrate the words of Scripture that say "… *with God all things are possible.*" (Matthew 19:26).

His message to others is: "Don't give up, no matter what happens in your life. God will never fail you when you put your whole trust in Him."

Chris has had many reasons to quit, but he continues to put his trust in the God who loves and cares about him, and who can do more than we can ask or think.

Don't Anyone

Follow,

or

I'll Shoot

William[3*] was raised in a Christian home and attended church and Sunday School regularly. In grade school, he attended a group similar to the Boy Scouts called Trail Rangers. At seven years of age, he played the clarinet and saxophone in a marching band, as well as playing with a pianist for the Christmas parties at school.

At age twelve, he learned that because both his parents had tuberculosis, he had been adopted from one sister to another. When they recovered, they wanted William back at home. There was, however, no cure for tuberculosis at that time, so his aunt officially adopted him. With only one lung each, both of his parents continued to live a normal life. William had a brother and three sisters who were all younger than him, but who never accepted him as part of the family.

He left high school after grade eleven. At that time, grade eleven was all that was needed to get a great job. His father told him to pick a trade, so at sixteen he took a course to become a barber. He started barbering, charging fifty cents for a haircut.

[3*] Not his real name.

He made good money and was able to have a new car every year. Three years later, he was able to buy his own barber shop.

At twenty-one, he married a girl he'd dated for two years. They had a daughter, who is now married with two boys of her own. This first marriage didn't work out. The wife and daughter moved to another city, and he continued to be a barber.

"I was taught that if a woman is good enough to marry you, then you carry out the part of the wedding vow that says till death do us part, and I still believe that," William says.

One day around this time, William went to a bank; he walked in the front door and encountered a well-dressed man robbing the institution.

"I want all the money, and I want it now, or I'll shoot," the robber yelled at the people behind the counter. He took the money and went out the front door saying, "Don't anyone follow, or I'll shoot."

William ran to see if he could get his license plate number, and then he chased the guy through an alleyway. The robber tried to shoot several times. After six shots were fired, William figured that was all the shots in his gun, so he continued chasing him. He was joined by another guy and the police. William got the license plate number, which resulted in the police getting their man. For all his help, he was awarded seven hundred dollars and a citation from the police department.

Things continued to deteriorate in his marriage. His wife got a job with a magazine company and started travelling through the United States, leaving their daughter with her parents. After more than a year of not hearing from his wife, William filed for divorce, which he says broke his heart. After three years of not seeing his daughter, his mother suggested that he get her and bring her to their place, and she would take care of her. Only three months later, the other grandparents took him to court and got his daughter back with them. It took seven years to get the divorce finalized, because his wife only came home three times within that seven years. She was finally served the papers on a Christmas Day. She was only home for that one day.

At this point, William's life started spiralling out of control, and he started drinking. Another relationship resulted in a new son, but the woman started running around. He experienced another failed marriage to a woman who did the same. These events did not help him get his life together. The first woman died several years later of cancer, and the second died of flesh eating disease a short time after they were divorced. The year he married the second woman, he started going to a rehabilitation centre. February 14 of that year was the last day he took a drink of alcohol. That is almost thirty-two years ago.

"I thank God for every day I have walked through this life as a responsible human being again. I also thank God I never started doing drugs," he says.

He was driving a bus and making good money when he met yet another lady who he thought would surely be the one of his dreams. She had been married before and had a son. They married and had a son and a daughter, but after five years, things started going wrong once again. His wife was running around, and another marriage ended in divorce. He stopped driving the bus, moved to another community, and started selling cars for a Ford dealer.

"I was down on my luck and was living in a bachelor apartment," he explains.

One day he visited his mother and met her next-door neighbour—a lady with a nice daughter, whom he started dating and later married. She had a son and two daughters. They lived in a run-down house that they later fixed up. William won a beautification award for all his flowers on their property for fourteen years in a row. He was married to this lady for fourteen years. One day they were told by her doctor that she only had three months to live. She was full of cancer and died almost to the day three months later.

William had not had much success with keeping a wife, but God is good and was not finished working things out for William. While at work one day, he had the pleasure of showing cars to a lady. They started dating and discovered that they had a lot in common. They eventually married. She had been alone for twelve years. She had two sons, but one had passed away in his teen years. The other boy lives in the same town as they do, and he has two children who are both in high school.

After all that William has gone through, life is good for him now. He and his wife are both Christians and are trying to live the way God wants them to. Until the day he retired, the only time William had been without work was for three hours. He'd always been either self employed or employed by other companies. God had been so faithful to him.

He suffered many consequences during his drinking days; he lost homes, cars, and many truck-loads of furniture and memories. His biggest loss was his four beautiful children, but they came back into his life around five years ago.

"It may be too late to mend all the years that have passed, but God still works miracles, and I leave every minute of every day to Him. I have a beautiful wife now, and both of us are trying to live our lives with God as our guide, which is the most important thing that a person can do. We love to attend the Salvation Army, and are blessed to have a great church family. We appreciate the Salvation Army because of their outreach to people in need, and we thank God for planting us there," he says.

He Discovered a Birth Certificate with a Name That He Didn't Recognize

Ken had three siblings. He was just a little boy in his crib when a lady came and picked up the four of them and took them to where she lived with her husband. They all stayed in that home for a while until one day their biological father came and took the three siblings but left Ken.

Ken's family had a farm, which felt like heaven to him. Children have their toys, but he had the real thing: tractors, combines, and live animals. He loved and enjoyed his childhood tremendously.

The family attended church, and Ken had an aunt who was very involved in many positions in the church. She was always talking to someone or doing something regarding the church. There was a policy that if you missed three Sundays, you didn't get a Sunday school pin. Ken had twelve. He didn't miss much Sunday school or church.

When he was five years old, Ken's adoptive family tried to talk to him about his biological family, but he wanted nothing to do with this information. He was their son, and there was no changing that. By the time he was six years old, he'd already been through some tough times. The lady who brought him to her farm as a small child, and who had given him such a great life, divorced the man he knew as his father. He had also lost three grandparents. He was left with a father who wasn't really his father, and an aunt who wasn't really his aunt, who later became his mother. He became a grandson to a grandmother who really wasn't his grandmother, but she taught him many great things that he would use later in life with his own children.

Like many young children, Ken became curious as he grew. His dad had a tin box in which he kept his important papers. When he was twelve, Ken decided to investigate and see what exactly was in this box. He opened it and discovered a birth certificate with a name he didn't recognize. He immediately found his father in the barn to ask whose birth certificate it was, and his father shared with him that the person who owned this certificate was Ken.

Up to this point, he'd believed that his dad was his biological father. This information started Ken on a downward spiral and a life of destruction that lasted for the next seventeen years. His family didn't want this to happen and had tried to talk to him, but he wouldn't listen.

"My Heavenly Father still has similar problems with me," Ken explains. "I still haven't learned to listen properly."

At this time, Ken was attending school in a small community, and he realized that everyone knew who he was except him.

In spite of all that had happened to him, God's hand was upon him, and He was using him in the prophetic. On one occasion at home while he was preparing to speak at a school event, Ken heard God tell him and show him that one day he would stand before groups of people. He didn't realize that the time would come when that would become a reality, and he would stand before people and minister to the glory of God and for His purposes. However, God had a lot of work to do in his life before that would come to fruition.

Ken's life continued on a downward spiral. He began hanging around with the wrong people, and it didn't matter where he was, whether at school or other places, he always found a buddy like himself who would walk with him through this self-destruct period of his life. He was only fourteen years old when he began to feel that no one loved or even cared about him. The people he hung around with started to invite him to do drugs and alcohol, and although there had never been drugs and alcohol in his home, he began to do both.

His family owned one vehicle, a truck, and when he was old enough to drive, he took full advantage of the truck. On Friday mornings, he would tell his dad he was going to the store, but instead he'd pick up his buddies and drink and do drugs all weekend. The truck usually wouldn't get returned until Sunday morning so the family could use it to go to church. Eventually they got a second car, and Ken rarely came home.

Ken's world was drinking and doing drugs with his buddies. He had no respect for anyone; he only cared about himself. During this partying season of his life, all he ever did for his family was bring them pain, but they never stopped loving him. After the death of his father and grandmother, the only family member he had left was his Aunt Minnie. She accepted Ken for who he was and never questioned what he did, but she was always there for him and always set an example. At a very young age, she began keeping a daily diary in which she wrote about the goodness, character, and principles of God, whom she desired to be like.

Ken drank and did drugs daily until he was thirty years old. Around this time, he started dating a girl with whom he stayed for six years and eventually married, but the marriage only lasted for six months. When it ended, he ran away. He admits that he still has a tendency to run from problems instead of facing them. Running at that time meant abandoning his father, who needed him desperately to help on the farm, but as he says, "It was all about me." He wasn't concerned about anyone else. He believed that the easiest way to avoid pain was to bury things very deep inside, which is still something he struggles with, because it's easier than facing the shame of the things he has done.

Having been brought up on a farm, Ken had a passion for driving all kinds of vehicles, but he'd never driven a bulldozer. While living in Alberta, he was asked if he knew how to operate one, and he said he did. He was told to get in one and move a pile of dirt. It took him a little while to learn the controls, but once he did, he had no problem driving that bulldozer. He spent the next few years driving not only bulldozers, but front end loaders and other large pieces of equipment. He says he would operate the equipment twelve hours a day for twelve days in a row, and he'd be high from start to finish. He thanks God that his foolish actions didn't kill anyone. He did cause an injury to one man, which he deeply regrets.

Ken soon came to a place in his life where he wanted to escape and wished he could die. He knew death was imminent if he didn't change his lifestyle. He couldn't continue to smash up bicycles, roll vehicles, and do lots of other stupid things and expect to live.

At this point he got into another relationship. This time it was a woman with a seven-year-old boy. Again, it didn't work out, but it was not his fault … or so he thought. He could never take responsibility for his actions. It was always somebody else who was at fault. He felt he was fine.

Soon a neighbour invited Ken to an Alcoholics Anonymous meeting, but he refused to go. However, this neighbour was persistent, and eventually Ken agreed to go with him to a meeting. During that meeting, an older gentleman said to him, "Ken, life is like a stepping stone, and each stone you step on has to be your decision."

Soon after this meeting, Ken felt the need to run again. He felt he was in another mess, so he decided to go home to be with his father, who he knew would help him. He only stayed there three days. His life was already in a mess, and the guy he was hanging around with hid marijuana in his camera case on the front seat of his car and didn't tell him. Very early one morning, Ken was crossing the border from Canada into the United States, and the border guards found the marijuana. He became quite scared, because he didn't want to go to jail again. He'd already spent time in jail for another offence, and he didn't want to experience that again. That morning he also had his dog with him. His dog was all he had, and he loved him dearly. The guards took him to a room, checked all his things, and then came back to tell him that they couldn't find a judge who was willing to come there at that hour, so they let him go. They told him that if he came back into the United States within seven years, he would spend the rest of his time in jail. Ken didn't know if that was the truth or if they were simply trying to scare him, but he didn't go back into the United States for over ten years. He wasn't going to take the chance of having to go back to jail.

Ken came home after that experience, but he still couldn't get things right. He spent Christmas Eve drinking and partying, but went to his dad's place for Christmas. When he arrived at the door, his dad looked at him and said sarcastically, "Everything seems to be going good for you." That night Ken went home and knelt by his bedside to pray.

"God, if I have to get up like this tomorrow morning, I don't want to get up."

Ken states that he's never had a craving for alcohol since that night. He figured the time had come to get help with his addiction, so he planned to enter an addictions program. They wouldn't accept him into the program unless he was willing to give up his other addictions, but he was unwilling to give up smoking marijuana, because he didn't believe it was giving him any problems, and he had no desire to give it up. Since he couldn't get into this program, he decided to start going to Alcoholics Anonymous meetings again and says he learned a lot of principles there about living right.

Ken had been living in Western Canada, but he eventually came home. He'd quit drinking, but he was still smoking marijuana. Around this time, he became interested in a woman whose husband he'd worked with in the construction industry for five years. Ken wanted nothing to do with God, but this woman sent him a Bible, which he began to read. He'd moved away from all the people with whom he'd been doing drugs and alcohol and got a job in Leamington, Ontario. His boss, though, was a drinker, but Ken was finally sober.

Later he met a man who owned a battery business, and because Ken had a dump truck, he was asked to take a load of batteries to Toronto. He knew this wasn't a good idea, but he did it anyway. While en route to Toronto, he got pulled into the scales. He didn't have a tailgate and he was overloaded. He also didn't have a sign saying that he had a load of acid. All of this was against the law. The man at the weigh scales told him that he was in big, big trouble, and that they would write him fines that he would never get away with.

At that time, Ken had been reading (devouring, really) the Word of God. Sometimes he would stay up all night reading.

He didn't yet know Jesus, but he was developing a love for the Word, and he credits what happened next to the favour of God. Suddenly, the man who had been so mean with his words came to him with a completely changed story. He told Ken that they were going home, and he should leave there and never come back. A little shaken, Ken headed for his father's farm. It was too late to go to Toronto now with the load of batteries, as the business he was delivering to would be closed for the weekend.

He decided to go and visit his Aunt Minnie. Even though he hadn't yet given his life to God, he began to talk to his aunt about the things he'd been reading in the Bible about being born again and about heaven. He was really trying to impress her, because he knew she'd been reading the Bible for many years, and he wanted to show her that he was taking some positive steps in his own life. What he didn't realize was that the Bible says in Romans 10:9–10: "… *if thou shalt confess with thy mouth the Lord Jesus, and shalt believe in thine heart that God hath raised him from the dead, thou shalt be saved.*"

Ken's aunt was very quiet as he talked to her. In all the years he'd known her, Ken had never heard her swear or gossip about anyone. He felt she was truly a saint. In all the years that he drank and did drugs, she never judged him, but just continued to love him. After his father and grandmother died, his Aunt Minnie was all that Ken had. In the later years of her life, whenever she was with Ken and his wife, Sharon, they would seize the opportunity to witness to her about God and would show her love and caring. Eventually she went to a nursing home a good distance away from them, but they visited her at least once a month and talked to her about Jesus. Miraculously, she eventually received Christ into her heart after they'd once again witnessed to her. That was a very happy day for Ken. They continued to visit her regularly for about ten minutes each time, and she would never let them leave without extending her hands and saying, "Prayer." Ken thanks God for His faithfulness, and he realizes God does answer prayer and blesses all who are faithful to Him.

After leaving his Aunt Minnie's place on the eventful day of the government scales, he felt like he needed to smoke a joint, so he went to visit one of his old buddies. They were sitting on his friend's couch smoking their marijuana when Ken began to share about the things he had been learning in the Word of God. He says that at that point his life suddenly changed and has not stopped changing to this day. He had an encounter with the Almighty God, whereby he fell from the couch to the floor and was given a vision of a drop of water falling down into a pool that was radiating outward. He got off the floor, not realizing that he had been slain in the Spirit, but as he looked out the window, everything looked different. The sky looked more blue than it ever had, the grass looked greener, and even the ground looked cleaner. Ken had received his spiritual eyes; God had saved him, and he still didn't know it.

He later went to the home of his step-sister who had a small baby. He walked in, laid his hands on the baby, and prayed for her. He was able to pray for this same girl again last year as a twenty-eight-year-old lady expecting her own baby. This was quite a blessing for Ken. This lady is not yet a Christian, but he believes she will be.

"I had been dramatically saved, but it took a few days before I fully realized what had happened," he explains.

Ken did face one bump on his newfound journey when his father turned his back on him and completely disowned him because he wanted nothing to do with this new man he no longer understood. Even though Ken's dad had gone to church regularly, he didn't know Jesus or understand the plan of salvation. He believed in God, but he didn't believe in being born again or being filled with the Spirit. Ken is not sure if his father accepted the Lord before his death.

Ken's life continued to change for the better, and things began working out for him. He'd always dreamed of one day owning his own business and being his own boss. He'd tried a couple of things that didn't work out, but after giving his life to the Lord, he experienced God pouring into him.

As a single person, he hated being alone. He'd always had the attitude that he loved children as long as they were not his own, but life was very lonely. That loneliness stopped when God gave him a wonderful wife and beautiful children. He'd been married before, but it didn't last because of many mistakes. Now God constantly gives him confirmations of his love for his wife. He knows their union was planned by God. Since his marriage, not only does he have Jesus in his life, but also a wife who fully supports him, and children who have stuck with him. He admits he is not the best father, because he doesn't have a very compassionate heart. One day his son who works with him in his business was leaving work and Ken said to him, "I'm sorry for being me."

His son's reply really touched his heart: "You don't need to apologize for who you are."

Ken has never heard any of his children call him anything but "dad," even as adults. He feels so blessed to have them in his life.

Ken says nothing in his life matters as much as his relationship with his Heavenly Father. The thought of one day being in the very presence of the Father for eternity keeps him going here and helps him look forward with much anticipation to the day when he will constantly be in the presence of God the Father and Jesus the Son in that glorious place called heaven.

Ken wants everyone who reads this to know that God loves them so much that he gave His Son as a sacrifice for the sins of the whole world: "*For God so loved the world, that He gave His only begotten Son, that whosoever believeth in Him should not perish, but have everlasting life,*" (John 3:16).

010

He Was Pinned

Between the Boat

and the Dock

Dorman moved from Newfoundland to Ontario in 1969. As a seventeen year old man, he enjoyed the pleasures that go along with drinking, drugs, and partying, but his life felt empty. There was a definite void in his life that was not being fulfilled.

He started working as a fisherman on Lake Erie and was living with a couple. The gentleman's parents were Pastor and Mrs. May, who pastored Wheatley Evangel Tabernacle. One day while attempting to get off the fishing boat, Dorman accidentally fell and got pinned between the boat and the dock. He ended up bleeding from his ears. That same night, Pastor and Mrs. May came to visit their son and family. When they saw what was happening to Dorman, they asked to pray with him. He believes that prayer saved his life and had an impact on the future that God had destined for him. However, after getting back on his feet, he started into the same old lifestyle he'd been in before the accident. He started drinking, doing drugs, and taking part in all the other worldly things that go along with that lifestyle.

He eventually changed boarding houses and started living with Leonard and Virginia Wright. Virginia showed him the love of Jesus in a way that amazed him. Even though she knew the kind of life he was living, she didn't judge him, but continued to demonstrate the love of Jesus. She often reminded him of how much God loved him. Even though he may not have realized it, this was exactly what he needed, because it brought conviction. This resulted in so much fear and torment that he felt like he was going crazy, but it eventually helped him make Jesus the Lord of his life.

One night in May, 1973, he talked to his girlfriend, Cindy (who is now his wife), and told her that they needed to get saved and start living their lives for God. To his dismay, she didn't see things the same way. They had a fight and he took her home before returning to the house where he was living. That night in his bedroom he fell on his knees and cried out to God, asking for forgiveness. God forgives all who seek Him, and as Dorman stood to his feet, he knew a change had taken place in his life. The next day, he got off work early and picked up Cindy at school. He felt he needed to tell her what had happened to him, even though he thought she'd be opposed to his decision. To his surprise, however, she told him she had made the same decision the night before after he'd taken her home. It was a very happy and exciting time for them both.

As time went on, Dorman and Cindy married, moved back to Newfoundland, and had four children. In Newfoundland, he bought a boat and fished for many years. He says that during this time he was very unhappy. No matter what he did, he was never content. He knew in his spirit that God had a call on his life, and that he was running from that call. He thought being a pastor was the most boring thing anybody could do.

In 1988, he moved his family back to Ontario, where he once again started fishing on Lake Erie. In the meantime, he began helping in the church being pastored by Pastor and Mrs. May. He helped with the praise and worship, as well as sometimes ministering the Word. He knew his salvation was very real, but he was plagued by fear. On January 17, 1995, while spending time in prayer and telling God that he wanted to live totally in His will, Dorman was reminded that God had called two people in his family who had been faithful Christians (his grandmother and his uncle), and now He was calling him to speak to the nations.

Dorman is now the senior pastor of Wheatley Evangel Tabernacle, the same church that had been pastored by Pastor and Mrs. May, who have since been promoted to their heavenly home. He has pastored this church for many years. He has also travelled to nine nations of the world, where he's been used mightily of God. In these nations, he has seen many people get saved, healed, and delivered by the power of God. God is an awesome God who will use all who completely surrender to Him in ways that will bring blessing to them and, more importantly, to others.

Looking back on his life, Pastor Dorman Pollett says he's never regretted his decision to give his life to God. Faith in the Lord has kept him going through all the storms of life. He considers it pure joy to have served Jesus and walked daily with him all these years. Little did he know the impact that prayer he prayed so many years ago when he placed his life in the hands of a mighty God would have on his life. It forever changed him! Below is Pastor Dorman's invitation to you, the reader:

"You may be able to identify with some of the things that haunted my life. You may be full of fear, empty within, wondering what life is all about, or thinking there has to be more to life than you are presently experiencing. Perhaps you are questioning whether there really is a God, and if so, if He really cares about you. Yes ... the answer is absolutely 'Yes!' He loves and cares about you. He loves you so much that He sent His Son to die on the cross for you so that you can be saved and spend eternity with Him in heaven. If you would like to receive Jesus into your life right now, just say this prayer: 'I believe God sent His Son, Jesus, into the world to save me. I confess that I am a sinner in need of a saviour, and I ask you, Jesus, to come into my heart and be my saviour.' If you prayed this prayer and believe that God has saved you, I want to congratulate you. Your life has changed forever."

You can contact him by calling or writing to this address:

Pastor Dorman Pollett
Wheatley Evangel Tabernacle
P. O. Box 25
Wheatley, ON
N0P 2P0
Telephone: 519–816–4994

She Asked My Name and Said, "I've Been Expecting You"

Corey had an excellent childhood growing up in a Christian home and participating in all the church programs. In his words: "I lived and breathed church." Looking back, he feels that he was busy living his parents' faith, but not really his own. He was known as a "goody-goody."

In high school, he started a Bible study despite opposition from some teachers and students, but he says that he was committed to the cause. In grade nine, things started to change as he began struggling with anxiety and depression, but he didn't realize what was happening. His parents would keep him home from school for a couple of days until he began to feel better. He was trying to find out who he really was and wanted to be, and he was growing tired of living up to everyone's expectations, both at home and at church. Up to this point, he had been very shy and reserved, but he quickly realized he could get lots of attention by being a trouble maker and the class clown. He began living a double life—one that would satisfy his church and family, and one that would make him popular at school. Even though he felt guilty, he maintained that lifestyle for about two years until he turned twelve years old.

Corey began sensing God's call on his life in grade nine, but he became very rebellious and wanted to choose his own direction in life, without the influence of church folks or, especially, God. In grade twelve, he began to form some very destructive relationships. On the eve of his final exam, he smoked his first joint of marijuana. From this point on, his life began a downward spiral. To support his new-found hobby (drug habit), he began stealing from his family and his university fund just to get high. This continued for over a year, and his family relationships got to a point where he was verbally abusing his mom. She eventually found his drugs and gave him an ultimatum—stop using drugs or get out.

Corey went to live with his cousin for a short time before going back home. Soon after, he was accepted into university and moved to the city, where things continued on a downward spiral. His life revolved around partying, whatever drugs were available, and alcohol. He also started experimenting with medicinal drugs, such as pain killers.

"Alcohol and marijuana were my biggest problems, with alcohol being in excess," he explains.

He continued to struggle with depression, insecurities, and loneliness. He began to feel that he was simply a burden to everyone. The more he felt this way, the more he drank; eventually, he began having thoughts of suicide. He would often sit on the side of the road for hours, trying to get enough courage to jump in front of oncoming traffic.

Because of his lifestyle, he began flunking out of school. He was also running out of money, as he was using his student loans for drugs and alcohol. On top of this, he felt unwanted by his family.

He had also developed a very unhealthy relationship with a girl. Late one evening, the girl and her mother invited Corey to go to Signal Hill, which is a very steep hill overlooking the harbour at St John's, Newfoundland, as well as the ocean. Their plan was to go for a short walk and enjoy the magnificent nighttime views, but the sound of a guitar playing caught Corey's attention. Always looking for a good time, he thought it might be a group having a party, but to his surprise, it was a little old lady sitting and singing gospel hymns. She asked his name and said, "I've been expecting you and want to tell you that no matter what you have done, God still loves you." She then sang him a song entitled "Teenager." It was a song his mom often sang in church. After the lady sang the song, Corey gave her a hug and left her. He tried to brush off the incident, thinking that his mom had set it all up, but deep down he knew that this had been a supernatural, God-timed moment. He says it had to be something supernatural to open his eyes to see how big God's love really is and how forgiving He is.

Later that night, Corey called his mom and told her about the incident with the lady on Signal Hill. He also told her he would probably go to church on Sunday with his roommates, who were all Christians. The following Sunday, he did go to church. He knew God had a call on his life, but he was still feeling very resistant. He says he didn't receive anything at church that Sunday until after the pastor had given his message and made an invitation. One sentence in that invitation said, "God loves you." Corey broke. The next thing he knew, he was standing and walking towards the altar, where he knelt and accepted Christ into his life. At that same moment, five hundred and sixty-five kilometres away, his mom was kneeling at an altar in her church and praying for Corey. A gentleman came and spoke with her, saying, "A prodigal just came home." That prodigal was Corey.

Shortly after his conversion, Corey decided to move back home, get his life straightened out, and follow God's direction. During the summer of 1999, Corey attended a Vacation Bible School where he met a girl, Charlene, who would become his wife. That same fall, both he and Charlene were accepted for training as Salvation Army officers. They were engaged a year before going to training college. Both trained from 2000 to 2002. A week after being ordained as officers, they were married.

Their first appointment was to Buchans, Newfoundland, where they stayed for five years. During this time, they had their first child, a little girl they named Arianna. Corey says he really enjoyed visiting the pubs and trying to encourage people towards God. He also loved building relationships with the men through hunting and fishing. Many of those relationships have lasted over all the years.

Their next appointment was to New World Island West Salvation Army church in Newfoundland, where Corey continued to build relationships with people outside the church as well as inside. He felt that in each church he was learning a lot about ministry and his own limitations. During their two year stay at this church, they had their second little girl, Abigail. Their third and present appointment was to Leamington, Ontario, where they have now been for six years. Here they would have their third little girl, Ava. Corey feels blessed in Leamington with his community relationships, especially being the chaplain of the local fire department, and in his relationships with new Canadian immigrants. He says that every day he sees people who, much like the old Corey, are broken individuals seeking direction in life and needing love.

Having three small children brings its own challenges and can be a real juggling act. Corey and his wife try to find a balance between ministry and family life.

"My wife and children are blessings from God," he says, "and I'm reminded every day of His faithfulness when I am with them."

Corey's message to everyone is that they seek God's direction for their life, because God sees the end from the beginning, and He knows what's best for us. God is faithful and loving and will never lead us astray.

To those who do not have a personal relationship with Jesus, Corey says: "Invite Him into your life. Find a pastor who can give you special guidance, and a church family who will accept you and love you unconditionally. Avoid negative, destructive relationships. God only wants what is best for you."

Author's note: Corey and his family have since moved from Leamington, Ontario and is now pastoring a Salvation Army church in Sydney, Nova Scotia.

He Told

His Wife and Children

He Would Never

Drink Again

Davie was raised in a town in Newfoundland, Canada, in a Christian home with parents who were pastors. He had seen many miracles. At a young age, he developed obsessive compulsive disorder. Things deteriorated when he started getting involved with the wrong crowd of young people and became very rebellious. At the age of nineteen he got married, thinking that things had turned around for him. He became a pastor, which seemed to go great for a while, but things began to go downhill for him. For seven years he seemed to be under a major attack.

A cousin, who was like a brother to him, passed away. This cousin had seen many miracles. His mother had been mightily used of God, yet her son died of cancer. The night before he died, a prophecy was spoken that stated God was there to do miracles of healing, so the mother was anointed for a miracle for her son, but he died the next day. For a few days afterwards, the words of the song "Blessed Be Your Name" were with Davie, but he was angry and had many questions. He knew, though, that God was asking him to listen to the words of the song.

Davie decided to go to a store, and there he met an unsaved friend. He realized later that this had been a "set-up" by God. The friend asked how Davie was doing, and then proceeded to talk about the cousin who had passed away. Davie told him he couldn't understand why God didn't answer the prayers for healing. His friend said he knew people had been praying for him, but then he said: "Maybe there was a prayer answered, but it just wasn't your prayer, Davie." Davie realized that God was using his friend to comfort him with the realization that his cousin's desire had been to go home to be with Jesus. God answered his cousin's prayer.

Even though he felt somewhat comforted, Davie was still hurting, so he started drinking alcohol. This caused a lot of conflict between him and his wife, but life carried on pretty much as usual. He continued to drink. After a year of putting up with his drinking, all the while hoping for things to get better, his wife walked away from the marriage, leaving him with six children to raise. His life was certainly headed in the wrong direction.

A short time later, he moved to Wheatley, Ontario, and continued his lifestyle of drinking. Often after the children were in bed, Davie would have a pity party and would sit, drink, and cry. Sometimes he'd pass out in the bathtub because he had been drinking so much.

"In the midst of my mess, God sent an angel into my life, whose name is Soraia. She took such good care of me, but I often wondered why she even stayed around."

He continued to drink for the next two years, and claims he was the most miserable person alive. Soraia would sometimes tell him that he'd be better off living for God the way he should be.

They eventually moved to Windsor and decided to start living together. Davie says that's when his attitude became terrible. He used to drink and be the clown of the party, but suddenly he'd become a very mean person, even to Soraia. He soon realized he had a big problem. He started thinking about his children and what his lifestyle could be doing to them.

"Even though my life was a mess, God still used incidents to assure me that He was there, just waiting for His prodigal to return."

One such incident occurred when he and Soraia got on a city bus. Just as they were seated, an older lady got on and sat a couple of seats behind them. She began to sing, "Because He lives, I can face tomorrow." The next day, Davie had a court appearance and would need to recall these words. Even though he wasn't living for God, he still felt that God was speaking to him, especially through the words of gospel songs... especially his favourite, which says that when we are broken in our sin, God comes and by the power of His Holy Spirit puts a new heart within us.

God continued to speak to him in many ways, and finally Davie surrendered. He knew that he had become an alcoholic. At one point, he looked at his wife and children and said, "I'll never touch another drink," and he never did. He's been living a sober life now for seven years.

Shortly after his commitment to God and his family, he once again moved back to his home province of Newfoundland. A little later, Soraia joined him and they got married. He says that even in the mess his life had been, there was a pastor who consistently spoke positive words over his life, despite what things looked like in the natural. This pastor was a major influence in his life and, along with praying parents and others, he was finally able to turn his life around. Later, he became a pastor and began fulfilling the call of God on his life. Davie feels Psalm 139:7 proved true in his life. It says: "*Whither shall I*

go from thy spirit? or whither shall I flee from thy presence?" Even
though Davie forsook God for a period of time, the Spirit of
God was always wooing him and longing for his return.

God doesn't waste any of our living. He will always take
our messes and our tests and make them our testimony, and so
he has done for Davie. He believes we cannot lead someone out
of a pit that we haven't been in ourselves. His desire is to help
bring people out of the pit of despair and give them hope.

His message to others is: "To anyone who is in the pit of
despair right now, I want to remind you that where you are is
not what defines you. You need to remember who God says you
are. God loved you enough to give His only Son to die for your
sin and the sin of the whole world. He loves you that much!
I'm reminded of an old song which says, 'When He was on the
cross, I was on His mind.' Everything Jesus did, He did for us."

His Babysitter

Turned out

to Be a Witch

with One Desire...

Tim was born and raised in London, Ontario, in a family of four kids. Tim didn't get to know his dad very well, because he lived at a motel that he owned. When Tim was eight years old, his dad hired a woman from Trinidad as a babysitter for Tim and his younger sister. His older brother lived with their dad. This babysitter turned out to be a witch with one desire—to destroy the children.

Tim wasn't allowed to use the washroom in the family home; instead, he was made to go in the yard where the neighbours could see him. This left him with much shame, which he would eventually be delivered from. When bath time came, he'd be put in a laundry tub in the basement. The babysitter would pour a hot pail of water over him, followed by a very cold pail of water. At this time both his mom and dad were living at the motel and had no idea what was happening. At Christmas that year, Tim and his siblings stayed with their parents at the motel, and everything about the babysitter came out. His dad fired her. Tim believes that all the abuse in his childhood was part of what caused his eventual drinking problems.

In high school, Tim started drinking and skipping school. He'd go hunting and fishing, so his father let him quit school and go to work on the pipelines. It was very hard work, and what made it even harder was his dad, who was a manipulator and kept his money. Tim's brother, who was a professional baseball player, didn't continue in his baseball career … also because of the manipulation of his dad.

Tim's first marriage lasted for three and a half years. During this time, he was continually drunk and couldn't keep a job. As a result of this marriage, though, he was given the gift of a beautiful baby girl. He began working at a store, but every time he drank, the managers would demote him.

After the marriage breakup, Tim went to a treatment centre in Thamesville, Ontario, where he was finally able to kick the drinking habit. He hasn't taken a drink since December 7, 1988—twenty-eight years ago.

From Thamesville he moved to Blenheim and got an apartment. At this point in his life, he had nothing—no clothes and no food. A lady in the bank gave him an overdraft so he could keep his apartment. The store he worked in gave him back his job, starting at four hours a week mopping floors and bagging groceries. Life for Tim was changing and would continue to change in momentous ways in the days to come.

"I'd been a chronic alcoholic, but there was a lady who worked in the same store as I did who kept inviting me to church."

He wasn't interested in going to church, but the day came when he felt like he needed to go. He missed a few Sundays before going back again, but this time as the pastor gave an altar call, Tim remembers thinking, "This guy is an idiot." Suddenly, the Holy Spirit of God came on him, and he found himself going forward and giving his life to God. Marie, the lady at the church who had been interceding for him for many years, saw that God was answering her prayers.

Life has never been the same for Tim since that day. Everything started to get better. He started getting more hours at work, but the best was yet to come. His life would unfold in ways he'd never dreamed possible. He started attending Praise Fellowship church in Chatham, where things would happen that would change the outcome of his life in a big way. It was there that he met his future wife, Ruth.

They dated for a short time before getting married and moving back to Blenheim. It was after Tim's marriage to Ruth that God brought a prophet into his life who spoke and prayed over him, telling him that his problems were not with the present, but with the past. That was Tim's day of deliverance from all the things of the past that had haunted him until now.

God soon called Tim and Ruth to start a new church in their community. They began with prayer meetings in the basement of their house every Friday evening. They also started having free Thanksgiving dinners for the public. They did all this for three years. Eventually they rented a building on the main street of the business section of town. After doing some renovations, they began having church there. They also started a regular soup kitchen as well as a food bank and a ministry of free clothing.

"Doing these things has been such a blessing to our church," Tim attests.

During this time, Tim witnessed many miracles as people dropped by with the very thing the church was still needing. They were walking in faith, and God was providing. All these things started happening nineteen years ago, and since that time, God has blessed them abundantly in so many ways.

Tim never understood why as a very small child he felt drawn to the sound of church bells ringing. He'd actually run towards the sound and sit and listen to it. He believes he understands now that, even as a child, God had His hand on his life. The sound of those church bells affected his young spirit in a very special way.

In the year 2000, Tim was called to be a police chaplain, and for sixteen years he has been doing this. He finds it very rewarding. In 2009, he was presented with the Citizen of the Year award for the town of Blenheim, and he also received the Queen's Diamond Jubilee medal for his service to the community.

We congratulate you, Pastor Tim! You truly are a servant!

His message to others is: "People may see you as hopeless, as they did with me, but there is always hope. God always has a plan for your life."

Pastor Tim can be reached at:

Blenheim Word of Life Church
22 Talbot Street
P. O. Box 2035
Blenheim, ON
N0P 1A0
Telephone: 519–676–8036
E-mail: tvjoyce.bellnet.ca
Church website: www.blenheimwordoflifechurch.com

The Doctors

Joined His Esophagus

to His Bowel,

Allowing Him to Eat

While growing up, Willis regularly attended church with his family. His parents also encouraged their children to attend Sunday school. He loved Sunday school and believes that the things he learned there have been a great help to him all through life.

At seven years of age, he accepted the Lord into his life, but at a very early age he drifted away from church and God. Whenever he did something wrong, he felt the conviction of the Holy Spirit. When he was nineteen years old, he re-dedicated his life to the Lord.

Things went well for a couple of years, but in 1984 he began attending Fisheries College where he got his journeyman's cooks papers. He also began to seek out the things of the world, and once again turned his back on God.

In 1986, he got married. The next year they had their first child—a little girl who came prematurely but was healthy.

They eventually moved to London, Ontario, where his drinking problems increased. In December, 1991, they had another little girl. She was also premature and died the night after she was born. This caused a lot of stress, which caused the drinking to increase still more.

They decided to move back to Newfoundland, where he went to work in the Department of Food and Nutrition at the Health Service Centre. On December 12, 1992, another child was born prematurely. She lived for only two weeks and died in Willis's arms of a brain aneurysm. He was completely devastated and didn't know what to do except increase his drinking to a new level, which was the only way he felt he could overcome the stress of losing two children.

Because of all the drinking, his marriage started falling apart. They eventually divorced but remained best friends. She eventually developed cancer. Within two years, she lost her battle and passed away.

Willis moved to Western Canada and remarried. This time the marriage lasted for five years. Before they divorced in 1999, Willis had a massive heart attack and almost died. The failure of this marriage and the ensuing divorce was also caused by his heavy drinking.

At this point in his life, he started feeling like a failure because everything seemed to be falling apart. He tried Alcoholics Anonymous meetings, but felt that wasn't for him, so the drinking continued. He had a good job with Alberta Health Services and got elected to various positions with the union there. Finally, things seemed to be turning around for him.

In 2011, while on vacation in Arizona, he began to get sick. After nine months of going to doctors, they finally diagnosed him with stomach cancer. The future looked bleak, and the only one he felt he could turn to was God. On September 13, 2012, he had major surgery. His stomach, spleen, part of his bowel, and part of his pancreas were removed. The doctors joined his esophagus to his bowel, allowing him to eat. What was supposed to be a three-hour surgery turned into nine and half hours.

During the surgery, God showed Willis that heaven was real. He had an "out of body" experience.

"I was looking down on my body and could see the doctors working on me. I started to go through a tunnel and saw a bright light. It was then my two little girls came and leaped on me. They tickled, cuddled, and hugged me. They appeared a little older with black hair and curls. They were loving me and laughing and giggling. Then I felt it was time to go, but they asked if I could stay. I told them I would love to stay, but God had a work for me to do."

After this awesome experience, Willis woke up in the recovery room. The nurses couldn't understand why there were tears in his eyes. The surgeon came to see him and told him that he had never before seen anyone under such heavy sedation with a smile on his face. Willis told the doctor that he'd spent time in heaven with his daughters. The doctor looked shocked, but then Willis told him his story. The only words the doctor could say were, "It's amazing."

When he recovered, Willis went to Newfoundland to enjoy the birth of his first grandchild, a handsome baby boy. He was in Newfoundland for six weeks before returning to Edmonton. One day God spoke to him and said, "Pack your bags. I'm taking you on a journey." He returned to Newfoundland and not long after was again diagnosed with cancer. This time it was bowel cancer. He underwent twenty-eight weeks of chemotherapy treatments. During those treatments, there were no side effects—no hair loss or sickness.

He started using a cane after his first surgery, but one evening while visiting Pastor Gord Young's church, the pastor prayed for him and told him that he would walk out of the church that evening without the use of his cane. He did and has not needed a cane since.

In June, 2014, Willis suffered another heart attack and ended up in the intensive care unit of the hospital, but when he went for a dye test, everything was clear. A week later he was discharged from the hospital. Soon after this, he experienced severe bleeding; his blood level went down 60 per cent, and he again came close to dying. His mother and sister-in-law came to visit him and pray for him. He felt very weak, and life seemed very uncertain, but again God intervened and completely healed him.

He still had challenges with drinking and became depressed. Life became a roller coaster ride for him, but then he went to Corner Brook for treatment and counselling for his addiction. There God spoke to him when a pastor prophesied that he saw a big door and flat land and God taking him on a mission. As Willis prayed for direction, he felt he needed to go to Ontario. He is so happy that he obeyed. Once in Ontario, he started volunteering at a food bank, where he met a lot of people who were completely broken … just like he had been.

Today, Willis is thankful to God for placing a wonderful woman in his life in answer to his prayer. He recognizes that God has brought them together for His purpose and His glory. Willis and Kristen married in August, 2016. They are looking forward, with much anticipation, to the plans God has for them.

God has given Willis a gift for writing poetry. The following is one of his poems:

My Comfort Zone

I used to have a comfort zone,
Where I thought I wouldn't fail.
The same four walls and busy work
Were really more like jail.
I longed so much to do the things
I never did before,
But stepped inside my comfort zone
And paced the same old floor.
I thought it didn't matter
That I wasn't doing much.
I said I didn't care for things,
Like big pay checks as such.
I claimed to be so busy
With things inside my zone,
But deep inside I longed for
Something special of my own.
I couldn't let my life go by
Watching others win.
I held my breath and stepped outside
And let the change begin.
I took a step and with a strength
I never felt before,
I kissed my comfort zone good-bye
And closed and locked the door.
If you are in a comfort zone
Afraid to venture out,
Remember that all winners are
Those who are filled with doubt.
A step or two and words of praise
Can make your dreams come true.
Reach out and grab the future;
Success will be there for you.

Written by Willis Pollett, 2015.

His advice to anyone going through struggles in life is that they should seek God and give their lives to Him. As he said in his testimony, "… *with God all things are possible*," (Matthew 19:26).

She Was Afraid to Go to Sleep

June says her childhood was the same as most children's. She's the second youngest of twelve children, so there were good and bad times. Like many families, they were quite poor by today's standards, but her mom and dad worked hard to provide for their children and did an awesome job. They lived in a small four bedroom, one bathroom house with more than one child sleeping in the same bed. Her dad worked extremely hard every day—doing labour work and digging up sewer and water lines with nothing but a pick and shovel. There was no equipment like there is today. Because he didn't have a car, he walked everywhere. He often walked four miles from his home and back carrying a big log on his shoulders. Then he would chop the log and use it for firewood to help keep his family warm. June's mother would have a meal ready for him when he came home, but he would get several small plates and share the food among the children, taking nothing for himself. June says she couldn't have asked for a better mom and dad, and she is thankful that God blessed their family with them. Quite often there would be fighting between the older and younger siblings, but they all made it through.

June was sexually abused as a child by people outside of her family. When she moved out of her family home at age fifteen, she got involved in drugs and alcohol. For a while she was drinking beer before heading off to school in the morning; she would carry the alcohol to school and hide it in her locker. When she was sixteen, she quit school and started babysitting for her sister.

At age eighteen, June joined her first rock band, where she continued to get deeper and deeper into alcohol. It was then that she met a woman, whom we'll call Kit, who was ten years older than her. Kit was married and had a two-year-old son. June and Kit spent quite a lot of time together, which soon led to a relationship. At this point in her life, June knew nothing about homosexuality and was not looking for that kind of a relationship, but it happened.

When the band she was playing in split up, June was devastated. Kit was there for her and promised that they would have their own band some day. Eventually, Kit left her husband, and she, her son, and June moved to another town. They started their own band and became very successful, but things soon started changing. They performed on the weekends and partied during the week. Every time they drank, they'd begin fighting; sometimes it was pretty bad. At these times, Kit's son would be with his grandmother, but June feels he still saw far too much. That is something June finds very hard to forgive herself for. He was such a great boy—very smart and intelligent and always going to church with his grandmother. June sincerely cared about him.

June and Kit were together for eight years, but during the last couple of years, June became very convicted of her sin. She desired to be saved, but knew she couldn't be saved and continue to live a life of homosexuality, drugs, alcohol, and rock and roll. That's when she started praying for God to help her. Kit knew June wanted to get back into a right relationship with God, but she didn't want her to, because that would mean their relationship would be over. June remembers travelling to a community where they were scheduled to play. As they drove, June started to look at the huge mountains around them and thought about the song, "God of the Mountain." She began to sing, and suddenly her tears came like a river. She turned to Kit and, between sobs, told her she wanted to be saved. Kit just glanced at her and turned away.

One morning, June got up to send Kit's son off to school, because his mother was working. She'd normally go back to bed with a hangover, but this morning she turned on the television instead. She started to watch a church service in which the gentleman was giving an altar call. She repeated the prayer with him and invited Jesus into her life. She immediately felt amazing.

"I was on cloud nine until Kit came home. I then went from cloud nine to ground zero."

When Kit found out what June had done, she was extremely angry and wondered how June could throw away eight years of their lives together without first consulting her. Things went from bad to worse. Kit knew it was over, but she didn't make it very easy for June. June not only had to stop living the homosexual lifestyle, but she also had to give up drinking, drugs, and the band, which she didn't find easy to do. Kit intentionally brought alcohol into the house. They had two refrigerators, and one was almost filled with alcohol. June feels this was Satan's way of getting her to give in.

Kit also made her feel so guilty about everything that at times she would give in and sleep with her, but she always felt so dirty afterwards. Eventually she gave in to the alcohol as well and lost all the joy she'd felt when she invited Jesus into her heart. Night after night she would pray that God would send an angel to help her out of her situation, because she felt too weak to do it on her own. Then June developed insomnia. For two weeks—which seemed like an eternity—she couldn't sleep. She was terrified to go to sleep … afraid that she would die in her sleep and go to hell. She tried to get sleeping pills, but her doctor wouldn't prescribe them for her, saying that she was too young at age twenty-five. Night after night there was no sleep for her.

One morning after Kit left to go to work, June lay on her bed—extremely exhausted physically, mentally, and in every other way. She decided she'd had enough, so she started to make a plan to end it all through suicide. Just then the phone rang. It was her sister telling her about a lady she had just met at her church. Her sister had told this lady a little of June's situation, and the lady said she'd like to help her. June was relieved, because she felt that God had heard her cry and was sending an angel, just like she'd asked Him to.

This lady, whom we'll call Jen, came to see June. She had her husband and another couple with her. They went to the park and talked a little. A few days later, she called and invited June to her house for the night, because she wanted to take her to a church service. Kit wasn't too excited about this, but June went anyway. When it came time for June to go back, Jen told her she wasn't going to take her back to the life she was living; she told her that God didn't want her to go back. June believed her, thinking that she must be right because she was the angel God had sent to help her get out of a very bad situation. June decided to stay with Jen a little longer. She called Kit and told her she wasn't coming back. Kit took it extremely hard and had to call and cancel two years of bookings they had scheduled.

It wasn't long before June realized that Jen wasn't all she thought she was. Because June was so sick and confused emotionally, she was very vulnerable and easy prey for Satan and his demons. She stayed with this woman and her family for four years. Jen's husband was away working most of the time, and Jen started brainwashing June. June still believed everything she said. She thought Jen was right about everything. Jen encouraged her to throw away all her pants and jeans and wear only skirts. June was only allowed to watch certain television shows that Jen agreed to. She had June lay on the floor face down for hours at a time, covered from head to toe with Bibles. The Bibles would be opened to scriptures that talked about demon possession and about homosexuality being an abomination … anything at all that she felt pertained to June. Jen told June constantly that she was full of demons. She preached to her 24/7, and her preaching was all about condemnation and how God was extremely angry and disappointed with her. Jen would tell June she was worthless, and that was why she had to treat her the way she did.

Jen also told June that she had to give all of her money to God. If not, she was a Judas Iscariot and would be crucifying Jesus all over again. June felt nothing but fear towards God, and she never felt she was good enough.

Eventually Jen locked June in a top floor room, which was a small, unused nursery. She spent many weeks there with only a big bucket of water and a mug. Jen said it would be good for her to fast and pray for a while and told her that was what God wanted. Every now and then she would bring her some bread … just enough to keep her alive. June doesn't remember much more of what went on with the fasting deal, but she remembers that when it was over, some family members came to see her and told her she looked like someone from a concentration camp. Her family went to the police, who told her there was nothing they could do because June was an adult. She would have to go to the police herself and make a complaint.

The abuse, including sexual abuse, went on and on. On another occasion, Jen locked June in a small room in her basement. This room had an old cellar joined to it. Even though she was still very sick, she remembers fighting to get out of there. She became very angry and started banging on the door and screaming, hoping Jen would come and let her out. She felt so lost and thought she was going crazy. It was a long time before Jen finally let her out of that room. As soon as June was free, she went to the bathroom where she had saved some pills and swallowed them all. Jen saw her do this and called an ambulance. They took her to the hospital, pumped her stomach, and kept her there for a week.

"You would think I would have told someone what was going on," June says, "but I didn't, and I don't know why."

When June was released from hospital, Jen took her back to her house, where she continued to abuse her. June was now at the point where she didn't even care anymore. She was actually wishing that Jen would kill her and it would be all over. She felt she had nothing left— no self worth, no nothing. She just wanted to die.

One day Jen decided it was time for June to move out. June had no idea how she could live on her own after all she'd been through, but she found an apartment and moved in. She was so lonely and afraid, she wished in a weird way that Jen was there to abuse her. She obviously was unable, at this time, to think rationally, so she devised a plan to end it all by using wire that the cable man had left when he hooked up her television. She made sure her plans would work, and then took the little money she had saved and headed for the liquor store, because she knew she wouldn't have the nerve to proceed with her plans without being drunk.

Jen happened to be driving along the road on her way to June's place. She stopped her van and attempted to encourage June to get into it, but she would not, so Jen pretended to call her mother and said she would tell her mother lies. June believed her and got in the van. Jen started yelling at her, and June realized she was not talking to her mom at all, so she tried to open the door of the van and jump out. Jen pulled over and started viciously beating on June. She kept tying to escape, but Jen was punching her over and over. June kept struggling and fighting her, trying to push her away. She finally got away from her and jumped out of the van. As she ran away, she turned around and discovered Jen driving her van towards her. June tried to get out of her way, but the van hit her on her hip and knocked her down. Jen stopped her van and told June that if she didn't get in, she was going to drive her van over the next cliff she saw. Feeling guilty, and afraid that she just might do that, June got in the car again, but this time Jen did not hit her.

One month later, June tried to kill herself with pills and was in the hospital for two months. When she was released, her mother was there and took her home with her, where she stayed until she was able to get her own place. She believes that God used her suicide attempt to get away from Jen. The doctors put her on several different kinds of pills, which affected her in a very negative way until she says she felt like a zombie. She felt numb! Often her mom would sit in front of her and would beg her to stop drinking. She'd be crying, sobbing as if her heart would break, but June would just sit there as if nothing was happening, with no emotions at all.

She started drinking and had liquor bottles hidden everywhere in her house. She also attempted suicide several other times. One day she decided she wanted to die, so she drank quite a lot of alcohol and took some pills. She wasn't pretending … she really wanted to die, but God wasn't finished with her yet. Her mom phoned her and got no answer, so she came to June's house and found the door locked. June's car was there, indicating to her mom she was inside, so she went next door and called the police and ambulance.

Later, her mom told her that the police beat down her door and found her unconscious on the floor, with barely any pulse. They rushed her to the hospital, where she stopped breathing altogether. Her mother told her, through tears, that the doctor was literally on top of her, pounding her chest to try and revive her. It seemed like an eternity to her mom before they finally got a slight pulse.

Before they put her in the ambulance to rush her to the hospital, the doctor looked at her mother and said, "I'm sorry, but it's not looking good. I don't think she'll make it to the hospital."

Her mother looked at the doctor and said, "Oh yes, she will."

Her mom kissed her goodbye, and the ambulance left for the hospital. During the trip, they lost June again, but they managed to again get her back. They did make it to the hospital, and June was in the intensive care unit, in a coma, for over a week. The doctors told her mom that if June did come out of the coma, she'd have major brain and organ damage and would be no more than a vegetable.

Fortunately, June had a praying mother and father, as well as other family members and friends. Today she praises God for not only bringing her out of the coma, but doing so with absolutely no brain or organ damage as predicted by the doctors. One doctor said, "I'm not a religious guy, but I believe there has to be a God who helped this young woman, because there is no other humanly way possible she would have come out of this coma, let alone have no brain or organ damage."

After being released from hospital, she went back home and continued to live in her little house she was renting. She continued to struggle with drinking and suicide attempts. She was so messed up from the four years of horrific abuse that she was unable to think properly.

One day June's mother suggested that she go to a place in the city where she could live and receive help. She agreed, went to the city, and stayed at a house there for five months. Although she did receive help, she relapsed while staying there. She decided to go to a bar for a few drinks. The little money she had soon ran out, so she decided to go home. She told a man she was talking to at the bar that she was leaving for home. He wanted her to stay and have another drink, but she told him she didn't have any money. He told her he had beer back at his apartment, and that his apartment wasn't far from the bar. She wanted more alcohol, so she told him she'd go with him.

They walked to his place, but June felt a little uneasy, so she said she would stay outside and drink. He had a car, so she sat in the car as he went and got the beer out of the trunk. He got in the car and gave June a bottle of beer that was already opened. She didn't think anything of it and proceeded to drink it. She can't remember finishing that bottle. The next thing she does remember is opening her eyes as she was being sexually molested in his bed in his apartment. She was terrified and very confused; her vision was coming and going, and she couldn't move. She tried screaming, but could not! At this point she says she must have passed out again, because she doesn't remember anything until she came to again and realized she was still being raped. Again, she was terrified and paralyzed with fear. She knew what was happening, but couldn't do anything about it. She passed out for the third time, but the next time she awoke she was able to move, as the man had passed out.

June got out of that apartment very quickly and just walked the streets, crying, for what seemed like several hours. She couldn't go back to the house where she'd been staying, because she'd been drinking and that was against the rules, so she went to a coffee shop and stayed there for a couple of hours. One of the workers at the shop felt that something was wrong, so she went to her boss who then came and talked to June. June didn't tell her what had happened, but the staff knew something had. She talked June into going to the hospital, where she was seen by a nurse who worked with sexual assault victims. She examined her and asked if she wanted to talk to the police, but June chose not to.

June wants to say to anyone who may read this: "Don't make the same mistake I did. If you have been sexually molested or assaulted in any way, do not hesitate to go to the police. You didn't do anything to deserve it. The person or persons who violated you deserve to be punished, so please report it."

It was very hard for her to leave the safety of that home, but she decided to get an apartment in the city and live there. She wasn't on her own for very long before she started to relapse again and began to binge drink. This went on for a while, until one night she must have taken an overdose of pills along with the alcohol. The last thing she remembers is feeling very drunk, and then waking up a few days later in the intensive care unit of the hospital. Because she was alone in her apartment, she had no idea who called the paramedics. She believes that it was divine intervention by God once again.

Sometime later, June started to experience a lot of pain around her ovary area and in her side. She went to the emergency department of the hospital, where she was given a cat scan. The doctors told her that there was a large tumour, as big as a baby's head, attached to her left ovary, and it had to come out. They admitted her right away, operated, and removed the tumour as well as her left ovary. When the biopsy report came back, it showed cancer. Fortunately, it was a rare type of cancer that stayed in a cocoon and rarely spread. Again, God blessed her, because she didn't have to take any treatments. She recovered quickly and was discharged and sent home.

Shortly after, June met Karen. They became good friends, but then it happened again. June found herself in a homosexual relationship for two years. This time it was an on and off relationship, because June was once again under conviction by the Holy Spirit of God. She is so happy today that He continued to convict her.

Karen treated her very well and was always there to encourage her, but June continued drinking, and her habit was getting worse. Every time she drank, she'd get extremely depressed and want to die. Now she realizes that Satan hated her and wanted her dead.

She attempted suicide once again and was admitted to hospital, where she spent another two weeks. This time she even attempted suicide at the hospital. She would make one more attempt at committing suicide, but God protected her just as He had all the other times.

Her drinking continued. She would drink at home and then leave and go to the night club by herself. Karen hated that she was drinking so much, and she'd stay up all night waiting for her to come home. Some nights she didn't come home at all. June finds it hard to tell this, but many times she got so drunk and high that she felt she had no control of her actions at all. She would often find herself in questionable situations with men. She thought that if she went with men, she wouldn't be a lesbian anymore. Each time she would feel so dirty the next day, she'd want to die. This went on for a while. June now feels that she was doing things to try to cure herself, but, of course, it didn't work.

Karen knew that June wanted to serve God, so she talked to her and they both decided they would stop living the homosexual lifestyle. Karen was willing to give it up, because she too wanted to be a Christian. That Sunday June attended a church that was just minutes from their apartment. The service had already started when she arrived, so she sat at the back. The pastor came and made her feel very welcome. June enjoyed the service and decided to go again the next Sunday.

The following Saturday night, June had been drinking and wasn't sure about going to church the next day. She eventually decided to go and again the pastor welcomed her. Very soon she started feeling convicted and began to cry. The pastor's daughter came and asked if she was alright. June told her that she wasn't, so the daughter took her into the pastor's office, where June felt safe to share some things about her life. She also told her she was a singer and played guitar. Immediately the daughter asked June to sing a song in the church service. June agreed but then changed her mind when she thought about the drinking of the night before. She feared they would smell it on her breath. She told the pastor she couldn't do it. She was feeling very upset with herself, and feeling much guilt and shame. The pastor looked her in the eye and said, "June, do you like to sing"?

"Yes," June replied.

The pastor then asked if she believed God gave her the talent to sing, and again June answered "yes."

"How do you feel when you sing God's praises?" the pastor asked.

June explained that she felt only peace and love. The pastor's next suggestion was that June go and sing for Jesus, and she did. That night, June gave her heart to the Lord. She feels that if the pastor had not welcomed her, talked with her, and shown her God's love, she would not be here today.

The next Sunday saw Karen attending church with her, and she too accepted Jesus as her Lord and saviour. From then on, they knew they had many people praying for them. June and Karen prayed every day to be totally delivered from homosexuality. They continued to share an apartment, and God was so faithful to His Word. At first it was a little difficult, but they kept praying and believing that God was going to completely deliver them both. Before long, June started feeling a difference, and things started happening for Karen as well. It didn't take long until they both realized they'd been totally set free from the spirit of homosexuality. June even found herself being attracted to men, which she had never been before. God is truly a God of deliverance. June and Karen were both asked to sing on the worship team at their church, which they attended for five years. During those years, there were many healing miracles for them both.

Some don't believe them when they share with others all that God has done in their lives. They find it hard to believe that God has delivered them both from homosexuality and that now they both still share the same apartment as if they'd never lived that lifestyle. They can only share the miracles God has done for them, and then it's up to the individuals with whom they share if they believe it or not.

They both prayed to be delivered from the desire to smoke tobacco. God answered that request as well. Karen was the first one to quit, and shortly afterwards, June quit as well. Normally there would be cravings and withdrawal, but there was none of either. It was as if they had never smoked.

June then started praying fervently to be delivered from alcohol. She would go all week without a drink, but struggled on the weekends with cravings. Even though she had accepted Jesus as her Lord and saviour, she was still having some problems with alcohol, just not as much as before. She'd started really well and had gone a few weeks without drinking at all, but then the cravings started. But God saw her through.

She went several months without a drink until she went back home to visit her mom. This time she totally gave in to the temptation. She drank, did drugs, and smoked again. She went to a bar and stayed until closing and got very drunk. She left to walk home alone. There was no one to be seen until a car drove slowly towards her and stopped. It was a man driving alone. He offered her a ride home and, foolishly, June got into his car. She was far too drunk and high to think clearly, and she wonders how she can even remember the things that happened after getting into his car. She wishes she couldn't remember.

The man didn't take her home; instead, he drove somewhere and parked. June told him she wanted to go home, but he sexually molested her. She couldn't believe this nightmare was happening to her again. He eventually drove her to her mother's driveway. She got out of the car and walked as fast as she could, thankful that everyone had gone to bed. She went to her room and passed out on her bed. The next day she felt awful, ashamed, guilty, and dirty.

God helped her once again to get back on track from yet another fall. Her visit came to an end, and she went back to the city and got back to church. The more the pastor and her daughter prayed with and for her, the stronger she became in the

Lord. She soon noticed she wasn't craving alcohol anymore. She didn't want to drink. Even seeing a bottle would almost make her sick. She was so grateful to God for completely delivering her from this awful addiction.

In May of 2013, June moved back home to live with her mom and care for her. Karen went with her, but soon Karen's dad got sick and she had to go home and look after him. After her dad passed away, she stayed to take care of her mom. June and Karen are still the best of friends. God not only delivered them, but brought them even closer as true godly friends. They are both truly thankful to God for all He has done for them.

To the readers, June has this to say: "If you are battling with drugs, alcohol, homosexuality, or feelings of rejection, abandonment, shame, and unworthiness, please know that God has delivered me from all this and more. He can and will do it for you if you will welcome Him into your life and ask Him to help you. He will do it for you because He loves you and wants nothing more than to take all this hurt, torment, and bondage away from you forever. God will do it if you ask Him and allow Him to love it out of you. I honestly thought, without a doubt, that I was never going to be okay ... that I would never see that light at the end of the tunnel that everybody speaks about. I literally felt hopeless; I felt nothing but emptiness inside. I just wanted to crawl into a hole and be left alone to die, but God had a different plan for my life, and He does for you as well. Please be encouraged that no matter how black and empty you feel, God is right there, waiting for you to call on Him. He loves you—He really does.

Here are some scriptures:

"If you confess with your mouth the Lord Jesus and believe in your heart that God has raised Him from the dead, you will be saved," (Romans 10:9, NKJV).

Come to me, all you who are weary and burdened, and I will give you rest. Take my yoke upon you and learn from Me, for I am gentle and humble in heart, and you will find rest for your souls. (Matthew 11:28–29, NIV)

"Trust in the Lord with all your heart, and lean not on your own understanding; In all your ways acknowledge Him, and He shall direct your paths," (Proverbs 3:5–6, NKJV).

And here's a beautiful promise from God to you:

"'For I know the plans I have for you,' declares the Lord, 'plans to prosper you and not to harm you, plans to give you hope and a future,'" (Jeremiah 29:11, NIV).

June's prayer: Dear precious Heavenly Father, I thank you for all you have done for me. I ask you to help and bless every precious soul who reads these testimonies. Please touch their lives like you have mine. Father, my whole purpose in sharing my personal testimony is that it will give hope to some hurting soul. May they see your love and how much you love them, and may it cause them to want you to save them and deliver them also. And Father, may you and you alone receive all the glory, honour, and praise. In Your precious holy name I pray. Amen!

Little Did She Know That

the Guy She Was Playing

a Game with at the Party

Was a Serial Killer

Dawn was born into a family of twelve children. Her dad was a hard worker who provided well for his family, but with twelve children to feed, times were not easy. Her mother often felt overwhelmed and left the children with the oldest sister and went out. This happened often, and Dawn would become frightened at the prospect of her mother going out and leaving them with their sixteen-year-old sister who, because of all the responsibility, would often get frustrated and take it out on the children by not treating them as she should. She often hurt them physically. Dawn and another sister seemed to be the two she hurt most, and Dawn could never understand why. She figured it was because the youngest ones were too young to hit, and the older ones too old.

From age two to twelve, Dawn was regularly abused by two older men.

At age thirteen, she was allowed to go to a concert because she promised she would stay with her sisters, which was the only way her mom would let her go. After the concert, though, she found her sisters talking to some boys. She started to walk over to where they were, but when she got there, they were gone. She went outside the stadium, but she couldn't find them, so she started to walk home alone.

After walking for about fifteen minutes, she noticed a man walking behind her. She could tell he was trying to catch her, because every time she stopped and looked around, he would also stop and look around, pretending to be looking for someone. She started to walk faster, and then began to run, but he caught up with her, grabbed her, and pulled her into a field of tall grass, where he attempted to molest her, but she was able to get away from him. She then ran faster than she'd ever run before, but he caught her by the time she reached the night club. He grabbed her again and pulled her into an unlocked van. She hoped that the person who owned the vehicle would come out of the club and save her, but that didn't happen.

The man started to abuse her again when suddenly Dawn heard two women coming out of the club. She recognized the voice of one of them as her sister's, so she started to scream out to her. Her sister heard and answered. The man let her go and ran up a back road that led to the mountains. Dawn's sister asked why she was screaming, and Dawn told her that she needed her to take her home because she was afraid to walk alone. She begged her sister not to tell her mom that she'd been left alone by her other sisters, because if her parents knew they wouldn't let her go with them again.

By the time Dawn was fifteen, she had started drinking and smoking drugs and cigarettes every day. She also started going out with a drug dealer and hanging out with people much older than herself. At sixteen she started dating a man who was seven years her senior. He was a heavy drinker, and she would drink with him. It was a very abusive relationship. When he got drunk, he abused her physically.

She finally left him and started going with yet another older man who was visiting from Thompson, Manitoba. When he left to go back home, Dawn decided to run away from home and go with him. It was a week before her parents found out where she was. They contacted child welfare, who sent her back home. While in Manitoba, she went to a party where she played a game with a guy. The next day her friend showed her a newspaper with the same guy's picture in it, stating that he was the serial killer who was killing women and dumping their bodies on the golf course. This should have caused her a lot of concern, but it didn't bother her or change her in any way.

When Dawn was seventeen, she left home again to go to Toronto with her oldest brother's best friend, but her brother was not aware of it. Two weeks after they arrived, the friend started beating her and even threw her down the stairs. She survived, but she called her brother to come and get her. He did, and he put her on a flight back home.

After she got home, she started dating the man she had dated before who was seven years older than her and a heavy drinker. She was with him for eight years. During this time, his friends and his father's friends would often try to abuse her sexually. She felt she was at the lowest point of her life and started doing cocaine and drinking almost every day. One morning after drinking and doing cocaine all the previous day and night, she wanted to end it all. After beating her again, her boyfriend slept off his hangover from all his drinking. While he was sleeping, Dawn reached under the couch, got his twelve-gauge shotgun, put a shell in it, and put the barrel of the gun in her mouth. When she reached down to pull the trigger, she realized she couldn't reach it. She remembers saying, "Dawn, you can't do anything right." Then she figured if she took all the headache pills in her bottle, that would do the job. But when she attempted to get the pills, she spilled them all over the floor. It was then she dropped to her knees and screamed, "God help me!"

She heard the Lord softly say, "You are better then this." She cried harder than she had ever done before.

Sometime later, she cried out to the Lord and asked Him to give her a baby boy to love and live for, and who would love her and never hurt her. She decided to be checked by two specialists to see if she could have babies, and they both told her she was 99.9 per cent infertile and could not have a baby.

She left her alcoholic boyfriend and started dating another guy her own age. After being with him just over four months, she found out she was pregnant. She did get her baby boy, but as the weeks went by, she noticed that he was having seizures in his sleep. She asked her sister, Patsy, who was a Christian, a lot of questions about God and about being saved. Patsy invited Dawn to church and she accepted. She started going every second Sunday. She also took her son to the doctor, who ran an EEG that proved he was having seizures. Dawn talked to Patsy about miracles, and she believed that God would give her a miracle if she could get two or more people to believe with her.

She had to take her son to get an MRI done to see what was causing his nightly seizures. Before leaving to take the baby to get the MRI done, Dawn called her sister again and asked if she would call the ladies of the church and ask them to pray at 9:00 p.m. that night, because her son would be asleep by then. They all prayed, including Dawn. She watched her son as she did every night, for fear that he would choke in his sleep, but this night he didn't have a seizure. The baby had the MRI, and when they were called in to see the doctor, they were in for a huge surprise—there was no sign of the baby ever having had seizures, and his brain was perfectly normal. This news impacted Dawn so profoundly that she decided she was going to serve the God that had healed her little boy. She gave her heart to the Lord on Halloween.

"The darkest night of the year was my brightest," she says.

Five wonderful years went by, and then she met a man from a town that was a five-hour drive away from where she lived. They talked on the phone for seven months, and then Dawn packed up everything she owned, took her son, moved to this man's town, and married him. It wasn't long before she felt and saw that all was not right with him. During their many conversations before she married him, he told her he had suffered from anxiety and depression when he was young, but the Lord had healed him; however, she could see that he wasn't healed. He started not wanting to go to church, and he didn't want Dawn to go anywhere without him. He wouldn't come out of his bedroom when company came over, and he insisted on burning her son's Disney books and movies because he felt there were too many witches, dragons, and evil things in them. This devastated her son and Dawn.

She tried to do what she could for her husband. One day she decided having another baby would probably make him happy and encourage him to get help with his disorders. The girl who, according to doctors, would never have a baby had a second child. We thank God for our earthly doctors, but it is so great that God has the last word in our lives.

After getting pregnant, things got worse instead of better for Dawn and her relationship with her husband. It got to a point where she couldn't take it any longer. She was getting sick; she almost lost her baby three times and had to stay in bed until she got better. To make matters even worse, the results of a blood test showed that the baby would have Down Syndrome.

Again, she cried out to the Lord and asked if her baby was going to die.

"Your son will live and not die; he will show my salvation," the Lord said.

She believed the report of the Lord. She moved back to her hometown and delivered another healthy baby boy. She kept in contact with her husband throughout the six months she stayed in her hometown. He told her he was working and was on medication for his health problems. Since those were the conditions for her going back with him, she again packed all her belongings and moved back with her husband. She decided to give it another try for the sake of their son.

As soon as she arrived back and looked at him, she realized he was not doing well and that he'd lied to her. He wasn't taking his medications, and he soon quit his job. They had to move in with his mother because there was no money coming in, but this was not a good living arrangement. Her husband started using the Bible to manipulate her and to play on her feelings. Both Dawn and her oldest son's nerves were getting bad. She couldn't handle all that was going on, so she left her husband the day before Christmas Eve. She had an apartment lined up and moved all her things into the apartment. Her husband continued to bother her and even threatened to take their one year son away from her. She was already getting depressed when her father suddenly died of a massive heart attack. That's when she broke and went into a full- fledged nervous breakdown. She doesn't remember much about the funeral or the visit back to her hometown. When she returned to her apartment, she started drinking again. She drank for days and would then stop for weeks, sometimes months, but when the feelings of loss, the emptiness and sorrow from losing her dad would sneak back, she would drink again. It came to a head when child welfare got involved. She started attending Alcoholics Anonymous and was given an addictions councillor.

Dawn eventually got back on her feet. She remembers asking the Lord: "Lord, where are you?"

She felt a warm hand on her shoulder. "Turn around," the Lord whispered. She felt that He meant for her to turn around and come back to Him, which is what she did. She still has struggles, but now she has the Lord with her, helping her through her struggles. There are many times she looks back and realizes the Lord's hand was with her all through her life. There were many times when she could have lost her life, but He protected her.

On October 1, 2015, Dawn was diagnosed with breast cancer. She believed God would heal her, and He did. That summer she was involved in a car accident, and He saved her life once again. Then her son, who turned nineteen on August 14, 2016, was involved in a very bad car accident on his birthday. Both accidents were so bad that both Dawn and her son should have been badly hurt or even killed, but they are both alive and well.

Dawn wants to say to those who read her story:

"God is a good God; He is a kind and loving Father who desires to help you and make you happy. He will set you free from all the addictions and hurts of your past. We are human and sometimes fall short and mess up over and over again, but God never turns away from us. We are the ones who turn away from Him. Just do what I did and turn around and give your life to Him. He will be waiting with open arms to forgive you and take you back. God is a God of love, and He wants to love on you, if you will let Him. All you have to do is believe He sent His son, Jesus, to save you, and invite Him into your heart to be your Lord and saviour."

She Feels Her Husband's Porn Addiction Forced Her to Rely on God's Love

Debbie was born in Kansas, USA, but presently lives in Newfoundland, Canada. She has one sister who is eighteen months older than her. She was a premature baby, and her parents decided to leave her alone in the hospital for four and half weeks so that they wouldn't become attached to her, as they expected her to die. When the hospital called them to come get her, her parents said they would come the following weekend. She didn't get the mother-infant bonding that is so important for babies. She now thinks she has spent most of her life trying to fill that unconditional love void.

On the day her parents finally picked her up from the hospital, her grandmother (who lived with the family) discovered a lump in her breast. She died of cancer twelve months later. Debbie's parents' focus had been on making her grandmother comfortable. Her mother seldom had time to hold Debbie. A toy held her feeding bottle, and visitors would burp her or change her diaper. When Debbie's mom finally had time for her, she was in deep grief for her own mother. She told Debbie how disappointed she was that Debbie was not a boy, that she didn't die when she was an infant, that she caused financial woes, and that she caused the grandmother's death. There was also some physical and emotional abuse. As Debbie matured and got into abusive relationships, she didn't recognize it was wrong. She just presumed that's how people were supposed to treat her.

It was easy for her to believe that the God of the Old Testament would punish or kill people who didn't follow the law exactly, because that was the kind of maternal love she had experienced. She knew God loved her, but she also believed her mother loved her, so love and cruelty were interrelated for her.

When she was seven years old, her dad had what was then an experimental medical procedure—open heart surgery on his aortic valve due to rheumatic heart disease. He lived another five years. One Sunday when Debbie was only twelve years old, she returned home from Sunday school to hear her dad yell "Mama" and die very suddenly. Debbie's mother often told her it was her fault that he died, because had she been a dainty, quiet, submissive, sweet girly-girl instead of a curious, intelligent child. Had she not plagued him with questions— questions he loved to answer—her father would not have died.

Her mother's view was that if something bad happened, somebody was at fault—and that somebody was always Debbie.

"Later, I learned that the person at fault is called the black sheep, and I realized it is a wonderful position in a dysfunctional family. Siblings who have roles that demand stability don't have the freedom to grow and experience different things. If they change, then the family dynamics fall apart."

As the black sheep, she was able to be a hippie, a soldier, a student, a runaway, a homemaker, a mother, or a holy roller Christian. She could move to another country and still remain a part of the family, because "Debbie's just being Debbie."

Because of the childhood abuse, she was forbidden to visit friends. She remembers once when she had a black eye, her mother called her friend's mother and said that Debbie was lying about how she got it. She said that if Debbie said her mother did it, the friend's mother should spank her for lying. That only had to happen once for Debbie to be very secretive about bruises and welts. Her vivacious, outgoing personality turned to introversion, and she still struggles with building healthy friendships. She is constantly working towards learning better social and relational skills.

The bad times were balanced with good times. Until the day he died, her dad read to Debbie and her sister every day. He usually read something about science, so that they would have a curiosity about the world God made. The readings could be about astronomy, animals, or worms. Then they would talk about the science and seeing God in His creation. He would then read a Bible story and discuss it before kneeling and praying. Her dad became a Christian the day Debbie was born.

"His childlike awe, reverence, and curiosity to learn about his faith was passed on to me. I love to learn, grow, and change," she says.

In other ways, Debbie's family was a very normal family with chores to do, camping trips, visits to her other grandparents, family games, drawing, painting, music, exercise, and the simple pleasures of being together. She was nine years old before her parents decided to get a television. They were always concerned that having a television would take over the family time and turn them into four strangers staring at a television instead of four people interacting with each other. Debbie feels that part of her childhood beauty was that her mom was still young and in the accumulation stage of life, but her dad knew his life would be short, so he wasn't trying to accumulate but was trying to build relationship so they would have good and happy memories of their time together. When he focused on them, he focused 100 per cent. No question was out of bounds; no silly statement was considered silly, but was looked on with dignity. In some ways, he acted more like a deeply involved mature grandfather who showed lots of patience, wisdom, and joy in his girls.

Since Debbie hadn't experienced the unconditional love that comes from the mother-infant bonding, she didn't realize she deserved that type of love. As she got old enough to date and eventually marry, she began to choose men who were unable to connect on a deep emotional, physical, spiritual, sexual, or social level.

Her first husband turned out to be a porn/sex addict. His sexual addiction was so terrible that he began beating Debbie because she wouldn't give in to his desire for her to have sex with other men while he watched. She was pregnant at the time, and one day he beat her so badly she miscarried. This convinced her to divorce him.

Sometime later, she got involved in a good Christian church and became a Christian. That's when she met another man who would later become her husband. He seemed like the perfect husband-to-be. He was a Bible school graduate, and from all outward appearances, a fine, upstanding Christian. They eventually married, but she very soon found out he was not all he portrayed himself to be. He was also addicted to pornography. His mother had supplied him with *Playboy* magazines every month from the time he was seven. He was short in stature, and his mother wanted to make sure he didn't become gay. They had two children together before his pornography addiction escalated into a sexual addiction. He contracted a sexually transmitted disease, which he then passed on to Debbie. This was enough to convince her to leave him and go through another divorce.

When she met her third husband, he already knew about her background, so he knew all the right words to say to put her at ease. When they talked about pornography, he told her that he would never view it, because it destroyed families, objectified woman, and broke down the moral fabric of society. This husband was a widower with three teenage children. They got married, and Debbie moved to his country.

Within two weeks of arriving, she discovered he was paying seventy-five dollars a month for online pornography. He told her his children must have stolen his credit card, because he would never do that, but the children were never disciplined for it. He allowed his children to view pornography, and even allowed them to have friends overnight and sleep together.

For Debbie, all this was very traumatic. She wondered what had happened to the kind, moral, understanding man she had dated—the man who would raise his hands and worship God with tears running down his face. Reading a book by Leslie and Lee Stroebel, entitled *Surviving a Spiritual Mismatch in Marriage*, helped her realize that this is not uncommon. God, whom she thought would be the foundation of their marriage, was irrelevant to her husband.

In her search to understand her husband's pornographic addiction, she found that a lot of women leave one pornography addict and then find themselves with another. As she continued to read books on this subject, she found that one author in particular did a great job of explaining why some women's backgrounds left them incapable of seeing the red flags in their personal relationships. From this author's research, Debbie learned how many of the wives or girlfriends of porn addicts were raped as adults, or sexually molested or abused as children. Debbie just happened to fit all three categories.

Her husband's addiction to pornography made life very difficult for Debbie. She already had a lot of things to adjust to: his binge drinking; her recovery from a mild brain injury, their new step-family, living in a new country, and not working outside the home. When her husband finally quit drinking, his use of pornography escalated. It was then that Debbie discovered he'd joined a dating site to meet local women for obvious reasons.

Debbie says her husband's addiction affected their family in many ways. Four of their five children had little to do with them. She adds, "Addictions stop empathy, love, compassion, connect-edness, and the time needed to grow healthy relationships."

As a wife, Debbie says she loved her husband, but she didn't trust him. He was always unwilling to do anything to build back the trust that his addiction had taken from them. At times, he would say he wanted to do something to rebuild the trust, but then he would decide that Debbie was controlling him, or, if it was his idea, he would say it wouldn't work.

"One of the problems that the spouse of a porn addict has to face," Debbie explains, "is that after years of being lied to, it's hard to trust our intuition, or even hear from God. We are so desperate to believe our spouse that we brain-wash ourselves into thinking they're being honest. That means that when we finally come out of denial, there's a lot of anger that we have to deal with because of the head games they played."

Another problem Debbie has is respect. As a Christian, she believed she should respect her husband, but she often fell short. She tried very hard to show respect, but she admits that at times she just faked it, because she found it very difficult to respect someone who cheated, lied, and refused to get help.

After years of dealing with this, Debbie finally found she could obtain a degree of relief by "getting into the Word of God heavy duty (a Christian term for studying the Bible). She began memorizing chapters of the Bible. She calls Psalm 139 a sanity saver. She feels that her husband's addiction forced her to rely upon God's never-ending love. She says his addiction had her running through the pages of the Bible to find peace and relying upon prayer to discover how God wanted her to handle it. It was only through God's grace and presence that she was able to stay in the marriage as long as she did.

"Although I hate that I've gone through this, I love the lessons I'm learning through the journey."

After her third husband knocked her to the floor and landed on top of her, she went to the hospital and then to a woman's shelter. She left her home with her Bible, her stuffed animal, one change of clothing, and $60.00 in her purse. Her six weeks at the shelter were a blessing. She presumed it would be women walking around looking morbid, fearful, and timid. There was some of that as they grieved the loss of their marriages, homes, and desired futures. Some feared their abuser re-abusing, and also the future. As they came to know each other, the fear and timidity left. There were some tears as they discussed what they had been through or how they saw their futures, but there were joyful times as well … times of sharing, caring, and laughter. Debbie knew she was healed when she could laugh about the abuse. Abuse is horrific and not at all funny, but laughter is good medicine according to Proverbs 17:2. It helped them know they were healing. Thinking about their future left them a little intimidated, but they also realized it could be better than they had known before.

Debbie was one of the few who didn't start dating while in the shelter. After three marriages, she knew she wasn't ready for another relationship until she worked on herself. It took over two years for the divorce to be finalized. If her husband was unwilling to participate in the marriage, it wasn't surprising that he was in no rush to participate in the divorce.

Two years after the divorce, Debbie went on her first date. It took her fourteen months to realize she was falling into the same pattern she had followed before. The new man in her life was typical of the other men who had been part of her life. When Debbie realized what was happening, they broke up but remained friends. She has since had a few other dates, but nobody has really impressed her. She has built a life for herself in which she seldom feels lonely, but she leaves herself open to God's will for her life, including a good man who will be compatible.

It was through her third marriage and its breakup, rather than the legalism of religion, that God finally got Debbie's attention. It started when she saw Wesley Campbell on a television show promoting his new books, the Praying the Bible series. She ordered his books and started to read them as soon as they arrived. They opened the Word of God to her in new ways. Campbell also discusses the history of Christian prayer, including meditation. Debbie had heard that meditation was bad, so she'd rejected it.

She downloaded Mike Bickle's studies on the Song of Songs. He was someone whom Wesley Campbell often quoted. Through Rev. Bickle's studies, Debbie started seeing a more compassionate and loving God who wasn't sitting on the throne wanting to send her to hell for any little blunder, but who lived in her (Galatians 2:20) and was in touch with her human condition: her struggles, pain, hopes, desires, fears, laughter, and tears. He loved her and accepted her just as she was with divine joy and love. Her old view of God as a mean God who was out to get her for not being good enough started fading, to be replaced with a vision of a loving God. These teachings helped Debbie talk to God about her love for Him, and it helped her to see herself through God's eyes as a beautiful, beloved daughter.

"My God now looks like gentle Jesus who loves unconditionally, both those who follow Him and those who don't." She says she has been helped to evaluate herself daily to see if she is as loving and compassionate as she should be to every person she meets, and whether or not she offers dignity to all. She also wonders about her humility or ability to see herself as a person living the human condition: struggling, failing, falling, rising up again, smiling, and saying, "What's next, Papa God?"

This growth has been instrumental to her Christian journey, because it helps her connect with others without putting herself in a place of prideful arrogance. It is helping her grow in humbleness, and helping her feel more beloved by God and more like Him.

As her view of God changed, He called her to a different denomination. She had only attended there a few months before going to the women's shelter. Her pastor visited her there several times and was very validating and supporting.

This church practises meditation, but Debbie, because of past teaching, was still afraid of it. Her pastor recommended several books on the subject, but Debbie felt she needed to do more research. After a year studying about it, she finally showed up at her church for Sunday night meditation. Since then, she sometimes attends faithfully and other times not so much. She daily practises meditating on the Word of God. It has been very helpful to her in sensing God's inner peace, even at times when she would traditionally be in high drama mode. She now tends to take life as it happens more easily and recognizes that when a car cuts her off in traffic, a telemarketer interrupts her supper, a rude person confronts her, or a cheque gets lost in the mail, it's all part of God's plan to get her to where He wants her in her faith. Now when these kinds of things happen, she can relax and stay in peace. She carries peace inside her that has been developed through hours of meditation on the Word of God. She now wonders if her last marriage would have turned out differently if she'd done more meditating in the midst of the storm of her husband's pornography addiction.

She wants readers to know that God is bigger than any of their problems. When she realized the truth of the words in Romans 8:28, that *all* things work together for good to those who love the Lord, and she saw these things being worked out in her own life, it became easier for her to stay in peace, to accept circumstances as they happened, to feel a deep connection to God, and to hold His Hand while walking through the dark shadows of life—even the shadow of death. There's a song entitled "It Is Well with My Soul," which was written by a Mr. Spafford as a ship he was on sailed over the very spot in the Atlantic where his three daughters drowned.

"I am learning it is not only well with my soul in the good times, but it is well with every part of me through the bad times, because Christ is in me, and I am in Christ. The perfect spot where I chose to live."